large
GOLD experience
2ND EDITION

TEACHER'S RESOURCE BOOK

Pearson Education Limited
KAO TWO,
KAO Park
Hockham Way,
Harlow, Essex,
CM17 9SR
England
and Associated Companies throughout the world.

pearsonELT.com/goldexperience

© Pearson Education Limited 2018

All rights reserved; no part of this publication may be reproduced, stored in a retrieval system, or transmitted in any form or by any means, electronic, mechanical, photocopying, recording, or otherwise without the prior written permission of the Publishers.

Photocopying: The Publisher grants permission for the photocopying of those pages marked 'photocopiable' according to the following conditions. Individual purchasers may make copies for their own use or for use by the classes they teach. Institutional purchasers may make copies for use by their staff and students, but this permission does not extend to additional institutions or branches. Under no circumstances may any part of this book be photocopied for resale

First published 2018
Third impression 2019

ISBN: 978-1-292-19435-6

Set in Camphor Pro

Printed and bound by CPI Group (UK) Ltd, Croydon CR0 4YY

Acknowledgements

The publishers would like to thank the following people for their contribution to this title: Lynda Edwards, Felicity O'Dell and Julie Penn.

Picture Credits

The publisher would like to thank the following for their kind permission to reproduce their photographs:

(Key: b-bottom; c-centre; l-left; r-right; t-top)

Image Credit(s):

123RF.com: Elena Shchipkova 173, Eric Isselee 173, 173, Paylessimages 155, Sam74100 167, 167; Pearson Education Ltd: Jules Selmes 167, 167, Studio 8 157; Shutterstock.com: Bryan Solomon 155, 155, Caimacanul 155, Delices 155, 155, Eric Isselee 173, 173, Iakov Filimonov 173, Igor Shikov 155, 155, Lara65 167, 167, Lusoimages 155, Scanrail1 155, 155, Tanjala Gica 155, 155, Urfin 155, 155, Yes Man 155, 155, You can more 155

Cover Image: *Front:* **123RF.com:** mihtiander

Illustrated by:

418 Neal (KJA Artists) 17, 19, 57, 59, 61, 63, 86, 89; Phil Dobson (Oxford Designers & Illustrators) 85, 88; Andrew Hennessey (Oxford Designers & Illustrators) 41, 43, 46, 48, 69, 71, 100, 101; Lisa Hunt (The Bright Agency) 49, 51, 58, 60, 91, 96, 98, 121, 122; Andrew Painter (Oxford Designers & Illustrators) 108, 109; Eric Smith (Beehive Illustration) 120; Tom Woolley (Astound US) 33, 35.

All other images © Pearson Education

Every effort has been made to trace the copyright holders and we apologise in advance for any unintentional omissions. We would be pleased to insert the appropriate acknowledgement in any subsequent edition of this publication.

CONTENTS

Introduction — 4

    Overview of the assessment package — 4

    Test format — 5

Tests — 7

    Diagnostic Test — 7

    Unit Tests — 19

    Review Tests — 91

    End of Year Test — 115

    Tests answer key — 127

    Writing and Speaking: mark schemes — 146

    Tests audioscripts — 148

Photocopiable activities — 152

    Photocopiable activities teacher's notes — 179

OVERVIEW OF THE ASSESSMENT PACKAGE

The Gold Experience Assessment Package provides a wide range of tests which can be used at different points in the course. Each level has:
- A and B Diagnostic Test
- 9 x A and B Unit Tests
- 3 x A and B Review Tests
- A and B End-of-Year Test

Assessment *of* learning or Assessment *for* learning?

Any test can be used either as assessment *for* learning or assessment *of* learning. Assessment *of* learning usually takes place after the learning has happened and provides information about what the student is achieving. The student is usually given a mark or a grade. You can also use the tests as assessment *for* learning by using the tests to provide information on how well students have understood new language or skills, and then providing them with specific feedback and suggestions for improvement as part of the continual learning process.

A combination of both types of assessment can provide powerful tools for helping your students' progress.

Teacher's Resources site

In addition to the tests in this Teacher's Resource Book, the tests are also provided on the Teacher's Resources site in both PDF and Word format. We recommend using the PDF version, as they are. However, if you do need to edit the tests, this should be possible on the Word version.

The audio files accompanying the listening exercises in the Skills and End of Year tests can also be found on the Teacher's Resources site.

The access code for the Teacher's Resources site is in the front of your Teacher's Book.

Versions of tests

Most tests have two versions: A and B. Versions A and B are designed to be at exactly the same level of difficulty and feature the same task types, however, the test items in each are different. For listening tests, the tasks are different, but the audio is the same in both A and B versions, making it easy to administer.

You can use the A/B tests in two ways:
- give half of the class A versions and half of the class B versions – this helps to deter cheating.
- give all students the A test and then use the B test either for students who missed the test or as a re-test or remedial work for students whose score shows they need a little more work on the unit objectives.

On the Teacher's Resources site, there is also a version of the tests adapted for students with special educational needs. See the next section for more information.

Assessment for dyslexic students

One of the most effective ways of checking classroom work and the teaching programme is through testing. Tests can show which learning materials work best for individual students, so teachers need to be able to select the most appropriate tests for their students. The two most important aspects of a test concern a) validity: whether or not the test measures what it is supposed to measure and b) reliability: whether it would produce similar results when used with a similar group under the same conditions at a different time.

When we consider validity, it is evident that tests written to measure reading comprehension, vocabulary, grammar or communication, will fail to obtain valid test results for dyslexic students. The type of reading difficulties dyslexic students experience in processing print affects all language skills and consequently will not provide valid information about their actual knowledge or skills. The same problem affects the reliability of a test. Obviously, if the same written test is used with dyslexic students and non-dyslexic students from the same class, the results will be significantly different for the two groups.

The Gold Experience Assessment Package offers alternative versions of tests for dyslexic learners. While the language content and linguistic level of the material tested is the same as in the main tests, a number of changes make it easier for dyslexic students to process. For example, these tests have a larger point size with increased spacing between the lines, and tasks which require multi-tasking have been reduced in complexity. See the introduction to the adapted tests for more detail.

Exam preparation

As your students are going to be working towards a final high-stakes exam, the tests also provide regular opportunities for them to try exam-style tasks in a low-stakes test environment, which should help them feel more confident going into the final exam.

We would recommend using past papers or practice papers in addition as you get close to the date of the exam. There is one full practice test in Unit 10 of the Workbook, and two further complete practice exams are available in the Exam Practice booklet.

Expected outcomes

We would expect all students who have completed the instructional material to score at least 50%, and the best students to score 90–100% on any given test. We have deliberately included more challenging questions in each test so as to help you identify students performing above the level.

INTRODUCTION GOLD experience 2ND EDITION **A2**

TEST FORMAT

The Unit, Review and End of Year tests have several parts to them. This helps makes them flexible, and allows you to assign only the parts you want to or have time to administer and mark. In addition to the tests in this Teacher's Resource Book, the tests are also provided on the Teacher's Resources site in both PDF and Word format. We recommend using the PDF version, as they are. However, if you do need to edit the tests, this should be possible on the Word version.

Assessment type	Quantity	Total marks	Timing
Diagnostic Test (A/B)	1 (at start of course)	100	45 mins
Unit Tests			
Language: Grammar, Vocabulary (A/B)	9 (after each main unit)	50	25–30 mins
Skills: Listening and Reading (A/B)	9 (after each main unit)	50	20–30 mins
Review Tests			
Grammar, Vocabulary and (A/B)	3 (after every three units)	50	30 mins
Writing	3 (after every three units)	25	30 mins
Speaking (A/B/Teacher)	3 (after every three units)	25	10–15 mins per pair
End of Year Test			
Listening, Reading and (A/B)	1 (at end of course)	50	45 mins
Writing	1 (at end of course)	25	45 mins
Speaking (A/B/Teacher)	1 (at end of course)	25	10–15 mins per pair

For practice Cambridge exams, please see Unit 10 of the Workbook and the separate Exam Practice booklets.

Diagnostic Test

The main purpose of the Diagnostic Test is to help the you identify any general areas of strength or weakness across the class. This will help you tailor your lessons to your class and maximise your time with your students. The Diagnostic Test will also help to place students at the right level of the Gold Experience series. The test contains 100 multiple-choice questions and is designed to last for 45 minutes.

To help score and analyse the Diagnostic Test, groups of questions are labelled by language topic in the answer key. Mark your students' test papers, and use the following guide to help you decide what to do next:

- If students get fewer than 10 of the answers right, they may not have the basic language knowledge required for this level. Consider starting with the level below.
- If students get 10–49 correct, assess their answers to check where remediation or extra help is required. Focus extra help on topics from questions 1–25.
- If students score 50–74, assess their scores and, if they score at the upper end of this, consider an additional oral interview to decide whether this is the most appropriate level for them, or whether they would gain more from the next level (perhaps with some additional help).
- If they get more than 75 of the answers right, consider starting them at the level above.

Unit Tests

There are nine Unit Tests, which test the learning objectives from each main unit (after Unit 10, students would take the End of Year test). These should be administered after each respective unit check.

Each Unit Test has two parts: Language (Grammar, Vocabulary); and Skills (Listening and Reading). Both parts have A and B versions. There is also a version of the A tests for students with dyslexia.

You can assign both or neither of these, depending on the time available. If you are including the listening test, it is best to run the listening audio first, and then students can do the other sections in their own time.

The tests will take approximately:

– Language: Grammar and Vocabulary; 25–30 minutes

– Skills: Listening and Reading: 20–30 minutes

The Unit Test as a whole is out of 100 marks. The parts of the test are split as follows:

– Language: Grammar, Vocabulary: 50 marks

– Skills: Listening and Reading: 50 marks

Review Tests

There are three Review Tests (one every three units). These are cumulative achievement tests, and so test the learning objectives from all units so far in the course, but with a heavier focus on the most recent units:

- Review Test 1: Units 1–3
- Review Test 2: Units 4–6
- Review Test 3: Units 7–9

Depending on your school year, you may wish to do all of these or just some of them.

Each test has three parts: Grammar, Vocabulary and Writing; Speaking. Grammar and Vocabulary papers have A and B versions, as well as a version of the A tests for students with special educational needs. There is only one version of the Writing task. Students do the Speaking tasks in pairs, and there are separate materials for students A and B, as well as a version for the teacher with questions.

As with the Unit Tests, you can assign all or none of the parts of the test, depending on the time available.

The tests will take approximately:

- Grammar and Vocabulary: 30 minutes
- Writing: 30 minutes
- Speaking: 10–15 minutes per pair of students

The Review Tests as a whole are out of 100 marks. The parts of the test are split as follows:

- Grammar and Vocabulary: 50 marks
- Writing: 25 marks
- Speaking: 25 marks

End of Year Test

The End of Year Test provides a skills-based test covering learning objectives from the whole course.

The test has three parts: Listening, Reading and Writing; Speaking. Grammar and Vocabulary papers have A and B versions, as well as a version of the A tests for students with special educational needs. There is only one version of the Writing task. Students do the Speaking tasks in pairs, and there are separate materials for students A and B, as well as a version for the teacher with questions.

You can assign all or none of the parts of the test, depending on the time available.

The tests will take approximately:

- Listening and Reading: 45 mins
- Writing: 45 minutes
- Speaking: 10–15 minutes per pair of students

The End of Year Test as a whole is out of 100 marks. The parts of the test are split as follows:

- Listening and Reading: 50 marks
- Writing: 25 marks
- Speaking: 25 marks

Marking the tests

The Language test answer keys include references to specific Student's Book pages for revision.

Writing and Speaking tests have detailed mark schemes out of 25 (see pages 146–147), similar to the Cambridge mark schemes, to help you mark consistently, and to help you give students meaningful feedback. If you prefer to use the actual mark scheme for the exam your students will ultimately take, these are available online.

Whichever mark scheme you use, it can be very useful to go through it with your students before they take the test so they know what they are going to be marked against. You can then refer back to these marking criteria and bands in your feedback.

Name: _____

Class: _____

DIAGNOSTIC TEST A

1 There .... a key on the table.
   A aren't
   B no
   C are
   D is

2 It was Tuesday yesterday. Today is ....
   A Monday
   B Tuesday
   C Wednesday
   D Thursday

3 I get up .... 7.30.
   A on
   B in
   C at
   D to

4 I'm .... a picture.
   A paint
   B painting
   C paints
   D painter

5 I love .... to the beach.
   A go
   B going
   C to going
   D for going

6 The children are all .... to the teacher.
   A listening
   B listen
   C listens
   D listened

7 We .... on holiday yesterday.
   A are
   B were
   C is
   D was

8 I .... by train.
   A visit
   B stay
   C travel
   D help

9 I .... fifteen years old.
   A is
   B be
   C am
   D are

10 You mustn't .... your phone in a cinema.
   A to use
   B using
   C use
   D uses

11 It's snowing today. It's ....
   A winter
   B hot
   C summer
   D warm

12 I .... a film yesterday.
   A see
   B sees
   C saw
   D seeing

13 I .... some money in the street yesterday.
   A find
   B found
   C finds
   D finding

14 My brother is .... than me at football.
   A good
   B worse
   C badder
   D bad

15 I am .... person in my class.
   A tall
   B taller
   C tallest
   D the tallest

16 You wear a .... on your head.
   A cap
   B shirt
   C T-shirt
   D skirt

17 I .... swimming on Friday.
   A play
   B do
   C go
   D going

Photocopiable © Pearson Education Limited 2018   7

DIAGNOSTIC TEST A

18 I'm going .... to Italy this year.
  A go
  B to go
  C goes
  D went

19 I .... got a cold.
  A am
  B has
  C have
  D to

20 Your .... is between your head and your shoulders.
  A neck
  B finger
  C toe
  D knee

21 My father is a taxi ....
  A doctor
  B developer
  C player
  D driver

22 I'm thirsty. I want a ....
  A meat
  B lemonade
  C pasta
  D salad

23 My computer isn't quick. It's ....
  A slow
  B loud
  C dark
  D small

24 There is a bus .... near my house.
  A centre
  B park
  C stop
  D shop

25 Don't .... your homework.
  A you forget
  B to forget
  C forget
  D forgets

26 I .... home at half past five.
  A usually get
  B get usually
  C am usually getting
  D am getting usually

27 What .... today?
  A do you wear
  B are you wearing
  C you wear
  D you are wearing

28 Mum .... sugar in her tea.
  A not takes
  B don't take
  C do take
  D doesn't take

29 I .... chocolate this month.
  A aren't eating
  B am not eating
  C am eating not
  D isn't eating

30 Sarah .... a banana when I arrived.
  A is eating
  B has eaten
  C will eat
  D was eating

31 Dad .... three new books yesterday.
  A has bought
  B was buying
  C bought
  D buys

32 .... when you left the house?
  A Is it raining
  B Was it raining
  C Will it rain
  D Has it rained

33 Mark wasn't listening when the teacher .... him a question.
  A asked
  B did ask
  C asks
  D was asking

34 .... to the USA?
  A Have you ever been
  B Did you ever go
  C Have you ever gone
  D Did you ever be

35 I .... Star Wars.
  A have ever seen
  B have never seen
  C did never see
  D am never seeing

DIAGNOSTIC TEST A

36 Jill .... never eaten sushi.
   A has
   B hasn't
   C did
   D didn't

37 Have your parents .... with dolphins?
   A ever swam
   B never swam
   C ever swum
   D never swum

38 What .... tomorrow evening?
   A you are doing
   B you do
   C are you doing
   D do you do

39 I'm meeting my cousin tomorrow and .... a film.
   A I'm going to see
   B we're going to see
   C I'm going to see
   D we'll see

40 I think we .... our car in the car park near the station.
   A probably leave
   B are going to leave probably
   C will leave probably
   D will probably leave

41 Mum says it .... colder tomorrow than it is today.
   A is
   B will be
   C is being
   D is going

42 If you .... a lot of sweets now, you won't want any dinner.
   A are eating
   B eat
   C will eat
   D ate

43 Joe .... very happy if he wins the race.
   A was
   B has been
   C is
   D will be

44 If you don't play table tennis more often, you ....
   A will improve
   B improve
   C won't improve
   D don't improve

45 Grandpa invited us to the .... restaurant in town.
   A good
   B well
   C better
   D best

46 Studying with a friend is .... than studying alone.
   A fun
   B more fun
   C funner
   D the fun

47 The city is .... at the weekend than it is during the week.
   A busier
   B more busy
   C busiest
   D most busy

48 How .... brothers and sisters have you got?
   A some
   B any
   C much
   D many

49 I don't have .... money with me.
   A some
   B any
   C much
   D many

50 There aren't .... good cafes in this town – only one or two.
   A many
   B any
   C much
   D some

51 How .... does this laptop cost?
   A some
   B much
   C any
   D many

52 Glen .... play tennis very well – he's too slow.
   A must
   B can't
   C mustn't
   D can

DIAGNOSTIC TEST A

53 You .... to leave now if you don't want to.
 A have
 B must
 C don't have
 D mustn't

54 .... I borrow your bike, please?
 A Could
 B Must
 C Should
 D Will

55 We .... to give the teacher our books at the end of the lesson.
 A must
 B should
 C have
 D can

56 Everyone .... eat five different kinds of fruit and vegetables every day.
 A must
 B mustn't
 C should
 D shouldn't

57 It's raining heavily – you .... go out without your umbrella.
 A should
 B shouldn't
 C have to
 D don't have to

58 If you have toothache, you .... go to the dentist.
 A will
 B should
 C may
 D would

59 My brother loves .... colourful pictures.
 A watching
 B painting
 C drawing
 D looking

60 Did you see that .... show on TV last night?
 A fiction
 B documentary
 C talent
 D programme

61 I hope the water is .... when we go swimming today.
 A windy
 B sunny
 C freezing
 D warm

62 Our football .... gave us lots of excellent advice before the match.
 A coach
 B referee
 C driver
 D guide

63 What time does the .... to New York leave?
 A fly
 B travel
 C flight
 D journey

64 Mum .... $20 for her new shoes.
 A bought
 B paid
 C cost
 D sold

65 We had .... in the front row at the theatre
 A chairs
 B numbers
 C seats
 D boxes

66 I've got some great games .... on my phone.
 A apps
 B websites
 C plays
 D matches

67 I was the only .... on the bus this morning.
 A rider
 B stop
 C ticket
 D passenger

68 .... on this link to get more information about the museum.
 A Download
 B Press
 C Choose
 D Click

DIAGNOSTIC TEST A

69 We must leave now or we won't .... the train.
  A go
  B catch
  C take
  D do

70 Alex .... a temperature yesterday, but he's better now.
  A had
  B felt
  C was
  D got

71 This movie is too long – I'm .... a bit bored now.
  A going
  B making
  C getting
  D coming

72 Sometimes it can be hard to .... time to relax.
  A spend
  B save
  C give
  D find

73 How often does your sister .... gymnastics?
  A do
  B go
  C play
  D run

74 Which websites do you .... most often?
  A surf
  B visit
  C go
  D return

75 I usually go home .... foot.
  A at
  B to
  C by
  D on

76 If we .... finish the exercise in class, we'll have to do it for homework.
  A won't
  B –
  C don't
  D can

77 I'm really looking forward .... in the school play.
  A appear
  B appearing
  C to appear
  D to appearing

78 Dad .... a return ticket for me yesterday.
  A is buying
  B has bought
  C was buying
  D bought

79 You .... get up early tomorrow if you don't want to.
  A have to
  B don't have to
  C must
  D mustn't

80 Mrs Cooke .... the students much homework.
  A doesn't give usually
  B doesn't usually give
  C does usually not give
  D usually gives not

81 Ben didn't want to take part .... the concert.
  A on
  B at
  C in
  D to

82 A lot of people are waiting .... the bus.
  A for
  B at
  C –
  D off

83 Look at that little cat .... the back of the picture.
  A on
  B in
  C at
  D of

84 I want to get rid .... these books – would you like any of them?
  A of
  B from
  C off
  D away

DIAGNOSTIC TEST A

85 I'm sorry that Jim didn't do very .... in his maths exam.
   A good
   B badly
   C well
   D better

86 I only invited a .... friends to my birthday party.
   A little
   B many
   C few
   D lot

87 They need much .... changing rooms in this dress shop.
   A large
   B larger
   C largest
   D largely

88 Jack was wearing the .... amazing boots I've ever seen.
   A most
   B very
   C too
   D more

89 It's a .... late to phone grandma now.
   A very
   B too
   C bit
   D some

90 It can be difficult to .... friends when you go to a new school.
   A do
   B get
   C take
   D make

91 Will you teach me how to .... that card trick?
   A do
   B make
   C take
   D go

92 Mum tried to .... the waiter's attention.
   A pay
   B catch
   C pull
   D bring

93 I'm a bit .... of money at the moment.
   A small
   B low
   C down
   D short

94 My battery is dead – I need to .... my phone.
   A load
   B arrange
   C charge
   D run

95 Let's leave now – we have a long .... ahead of us.
   A travel
   B transport
   C go
   D journey

96 Liverpool is a large city on the west .... of the UK.
   A sea
   B coast
   C beach
   D place

97 Please don't drop litter on the pavement – put it in the ....
   A can
   B tin
   C bin
   D box

98 You need to read and listen to a lot of English if you want to .... your language skills.
   A improve
   B grow
   C move
   D connect

99 My grandparents gave me the money for my .... when I flew to Australia last year.
   A payment
   B fare
   C bill
   D cost

100 My feet have grown – these shoes don't .... me any longer.
    A put
    B fit
    C use
    D wear

Total: 100

DIAGNOSTIC TEST B

1 There .... a nice café over there.
   A it's
   B has
   C is
   D are

2 It was Tuesday yesterday. Tomorrow is ....
   A Monday
   B Tuesday
   C Wednesday
   D Thursday

3 My birthday is .... August.
   A on
   B in
   C at
   D to

4 I'm .... a video game.
   A play
   B playing
   C plays
   D player

5 I love .... TV.
   A watch
   B watches
   C watching
   D a watch

6 The children are all .... a book.
   A read
   B reads
   C reading
   D reader

7 I .... on holiday yesterday.
   A are
   B were
   C is
   D was

8 I .... by bus to school every day.
   A went
   B goes
   C go
   D going

9 He .... fifteen years old.
   A is
   B be
   C am
   D are

10 You mustn't .... food in a cinema.
   A to eat
   B eat
   C eating
   D eats

11 It's hot today. It's ....
   A winter
   B cold
   C summer
   D snowy

12 I .... a book yesterday.
   A read
   B reads
   C reading
   D reader

13 I .... a film yesterday.
   A see
   B saw
   C sees
   D seeing

14 My brother is .... than me at football.
   A good
   B worse
   C not good
   D bad

15 I am .... person in my class.
   A young
   B the youngest
   C youngest
   D the younger

16 You wear .... on your legs.
   A trousers
   B a shirt
   C a T-shirt
   D a cap

17 I .... football on Friday.
   A play
   B do
   C go
   D going

18 I'm going .... a film tonight
   A watch
   B to watch
   C watched
   D watching

DIAGNOSTIC TEST B

19 She .... got a toothache.
   A am
   B has
   C have
   D to

20 Your .... is on your foot..
   A neck
   B finger
   C toe
   D knee

21 My father is a tennis ....
   A doctor
   B developer
   C player
   D driver

22 I'm hungry. I want a ....
   A water
   B lemonade
   C sandwich
   D milk shake

23 My computer isn't slow. It's ....
   A quick
   B loud
   C dark
   D small

24 There is a train .... near my house.
   A centre
   B station
   C stop
   D shop

25 Please .... the window.
   A you open
   B to open
   C open
   D opens

26 What .... at the moment?
   A you read
   B you are reading
   C do you read
   D are you reading

27 My brothers .... playing football today.
   A aren't playing
   B am not playing
   C are playing not
   D isn't playing

28 Sasha .... up at six thirty.
   A is always getting
   B is getting always
   C always gets
   D gets always

29 I .... coffee.
   A not drink
   B don't drink
   C does drink
   D doesn't drink

30 I .... a lot of money yesterday.
   A spend
   B spent
   C have spent
   D was spending

31 The girls .... in the garden when we got home.
   A are playing
   B were playing
   C have played
   D will play

32 I wasn't doing my homework when Dad .... me.
   A phoned
   B has phoned
   C phones
   D was phoning

33 .... when you left school?
   A Is it snowing
   B Will it snow
   C Was it snowing
   D Has it snowed

34 My dad .... never ridden a motorbike.
   A has
   B hasn't
   C did
   D didn't

35 .... to China?
   A Did you ever go
   B Have you ever been
   C Did you ever be
   D Have you ever

36 Have your friends .... on a sleepover at your house?
   A never been
   B never been
   C ever been
   D ever going

DIAGNOSTIC TEST B

37 I .... *War and Peace*.
  A did never read
  B have ever read
  C am never reading
  D have never read

38 I'm going to my friend's house tomorrow and .... her new computer game.
  A I'm going to play
  B we're going to play
  C I'm playing
  D we'll play

39 What .... this summer?
  A you are doing
  B are you doing
  C you do
  D do you do

40 Grandma says it .... warmer tomorrow than it is today.
  A is
  B is being
  C is going
  D will be

41 I think I .... a chess club next year.
  A will probably join
  B are going to join probably
  C probably join
  D will join probably

42 If our football team doesn't practise more often, it ....
  A will improve
  B won't improve
  C doesn't improve
  D improves

43 If you .... all your money now, you'll be sorry tomorrow.
  A are spending
  B spend
  C will spend
  D spent

44 I .... very happy if I win a prize.
  A was
  B has been
  C will be
  D is

45 The shops are .... at the weekend than they are during the week.
  A more busy
  B busiest
  C busier
  D most busy

46 What do you think is the .... park in this town?
  A well
  B good
  C best
  D better

47 I think skateboarding is .... than snowboarding.
  A more fun
  B fun
  C the fun
  D funner

48 How .... do these trainers cost?
  A some
  B any
  C much
  D many

49 There aren't .... places to eat near here – only one or two.
  A any
  B much
  C some
  D many

50 There isn't .... milk in the fridge.
  A some
  B no
  C much
  D many

51 How .... friends have you got?
  A some
  B many
  C any
  D much

52 .... you lend me a pen, please?
  A Do
  B Could
  C Must
  D Should

DIAGNOSTIC TEST B

53 Ruby .... to stay if she doesn't want to.
 A doesn't have to
 B must
 C has to
 D mustn't

54 You .... to finish your homework before Friday.
 A must
 B should
 C have
 D can

55 I .... run very fast – my legs are too short.
 A must
 B mustn't
 C can
 D can't

56 It's very cold today – you .... go out without a scarf.
 A should
 B shouldn't
 C don't have to
 D have to

57 If Orla has toothache, she .... go to the dentist.
 A will
 B may
 C would
 D should

58 No one .... eat pizza every day.
 A must
 B should
 C mustn't
 D shouldn't

59 Do you enjoy watching .... shows on TV?
 A talent
 B fiction
 C programme
 D documentary

60 My tennis .... has really helped me improve my game.
 A referee
 B driver
 C guide
 D coach

61 Uncle Dan's .... leaves at 8.30 tomorrow.
 A fly
 B flight
 C journey
 D travel

62 The water was lovely and .... when we went swimming today.
 A windy
 B warm
 C sunny
 D freezing

63 I like .... colourful pictures.
 A looking
 B doing
 C painting
 D learning

64 There was only two other .... with me on the bus this morning.
 A riders
 B passengers
 C stops
 D tickets

65 Helena's got a great new music .... on her phone.
 A play
 B website
 C app
 D song

66 I .... fifteen euros for my concert ticket.
 A bought
 B cost
 C paid
 D sold

67 Our .... were in the front row at the theatre
 A chairs
 B boxes
 C numbers
 D seats

68 Terry should leave now or he won't .... the train.
 A catch
 B do
 D go
 C take

69 Clare .... a temperature this morning, but she's OK now.
 A felt
 B had
 C got
 D was

16

DIAGNOSTIC TEST B

70 .... on this link to get more information about the museum.
   A Download
   B Click
   C Press
   D Choose

71 My brother .... judo every Thursday after school.
   A runs
   B does
   C plays
   D goes

72 This story is too difficult for the class – they're .... a bit bored now.
   A coming
   B going
   C getting
   D making

73 There are a few websites that I .... almost every day.
   A visit
   B go
   C surf
   D return

74 Tom always goes to work .... foot.
   A at
   B on
   C by
   D to

75 People usually .... time to relax at the weekend.
   A save
   B look
   C find
   D give

76 Hannah .... for our meal last night.
   A is paying
   B has paid
   C paid
   D was paying

77 We .... much homework from Mrs Cooke.
   A don't get usually
   B do usually not get
   C usually get not
   D don't usually get

78 The children .... wear school uniform tomorrow if they don't want to.
   A have to
   B must
   C don't have to
   D mustn't

79 We're all looking forward .... you soon.
   A to see
   B to seeing
   C see
   D seeing

80 Ken won't do well in his test, if he .... spend more time studying.
   A won't
   B doesn't
   C can
   D –

81 There is a car park .... the back of the restaurant.
   A at
   B in
   C on
   D of

82 How can we get rid .... our old plastic bottles?
   A away
   B of
   C out
   B from

83 Don't wait .... me – I'll come later.
   A at
   B up
   C –
   D for

84 Ben didn't want to take part .... the concert.
   A on
   B in
   C at
   D to

85 I'd love to have a much .... bedroom.
   A large
   B larger
   C largest
   D largely

DIAGNOSTIC TEST B

86 My little cousin is only four and she can't swim very .... yet.
 A good
 B badly
 C better
 D well

87 There were only a .... mistakes in my homework.
 A little
 B few
 C many
 D lot

88 It's a .... late to phone grandma now.
 A very
 B too
 C some
 D bit

89 Katy played the .... beautiful song I've ever heard.
 A very
 B most
 C too
 D more

90 My battery is dead – where can I .... my phone?
 A run
 B charge
 C arrange
 D load

91 Emma quickly .... friends at her new school.
 A did
 B brought
 C made
 D took

92 Can you lend me £10, please? I'm a bit .... of money at the moment.
 A small
 B low
 C short
 D down

93 Is that card trick difficult to .... ?
 A make
 B take
 C do
 D go

94 If you can .... the waiter's attention, I'll order some ice cream.
 A catch
 B pay
 C pull
 D bring

95 There are some wonderful beaches on the west .... of Ireland.
 A sea
 B border
 C place
 D coast

96 Do you have a long .... to school every day?
 A transport
 B travel
 C journey
 D go

97 This dress doesn't .... me any longer – it's much too small.
 A put
 B use
 C fit
 D wear

98 The return .... to London on a weekend flight is £150.
 A bill
 B payment
 C fare
 D cost

99 Please put all your rubbish in the .... at the end of the street.
 A bin
 B can
 C tin
 D box

100 Your English will .... a lot if you read something in English every day.
 A grow
 B improve
 C connect
 D move

Total: 100

UNIT 1: LANGUAGE TEST A

VOCABULARY

Task 1
Write the *-ing* form of the verbs.
1 bake   ....
2 fish   ....
3 paint ....
4 sing   ....

[4]

Task 2
Complete the sentences with the nouns from Task 1.
5 I love .... with my friends. We sometimes put our music on our school website.
6 Gary goes .... on Sunday with his dad. They sit in a boat all day.
7 My sister loves .... This is her cake!
8 Jacky's hobby is .... Here's a picture of her dog. It's amazing!

[4]

Task 3
Match the sentence beginnings (9–15) with the endings (A–G).
9   I usually listen   ....
10 My friend Ewan loves music and plays   ....
11 My sister often goes on   ....
12 My younger brother loves watching   ....
13 I like films and usually go   ....
14 My dad and I sometimes play   ....
15 My main hobby is collecting   ....

A the guitar in a group with his friends.
B cards when we're bored on holiday.
C comics from the USA.
D a sleepover at her friend's house.
E cartoons on TV.
F to the radio in the car.
G to the cinema with my friend on Saturdays.

[7]

Task 4
Choose the correct answer (A, B or C).
16 My brother .... video games with his friends after school and he usually wins!
    A reads   B collects   C plays
17 I love .... and I often go into the garden with my pencil and do pictures of the trees.
    A dancing   B drawing   C collecting
18 My best friend is brilliant .... dancing.
    A on   B for   C at
19 Do you like .... in a tent?
    A baking   B singing   C camping
20 My sister .... in a group at school.
    A fishes   B sings   C listens
21 I don't enjoy watching .... on TV.
    A cartoons   B comics   C cards
22 I sometimes .... videos.
    A go   B watch   C listen
23 I don't often .... comics.
    A watch   B look   C read
24 I play a lot of .... in my free time.
    A video games   B football   C guitar
25 I'm not good .... singing.
    A with   B on   C at

[10]

Photocopiable © Pearson Education Limited 2018   19

UNIT 1: LANGUAGE TEST A

GRAMMAR

Task 1
Complete the sentences with the present simple form of the verbs in brackets.
26 I .... (not / want) to go to the cinema today. I'm really tired.
27 .... (you / go) on sleepovers very often?
28 Our teacher .... (speak) lots of different languages.
29 Eva .... (not / do) her homework in the evenings.
30 My friends often .... (watch) videos after lessons at school.
31 Katy .... (not / like) listening to pop music.
32 How often .... (your mum / go) shopping?
33 .... (your brother / win?) win prizes for his paintings?
34 We .... (not / play) football on Fridays.
35 .... (you / want) to play cards?

10

Task 2
Complete each sentence with *much* or *many*.
36 There aren't .... people in the cinema today – about ten or twenty.
37 How .... money have you got? Maybe we can go shopping!
38 I'm sorry, but I haven't got .... free time this week.
39 How .... books have you got in this bag? It's very heavy!
40 We don't have .... homework tonight. Only one exercise!

5

Task 3
Put the words in the correct order to make sentences.
41 She / feels / before a competition / always / nervous / .

....

42 Paul / with his camera / takes / never / .

....

43 I / often / not / am / late / for school / .

....

44 Anna / speaks / usually / quietly / .

....

45 drink coffee / don't / for breakfast / always / I / .

....

10

Total: 50

UNIT 1: LANGUAGE TEST B

VOCABULARY

Task 1
Write the -ing form of the verbs.
1 draw ....
2 read ....
3 dance ....
4 camp ....

[4]

Task 2
Complete the sentences with the nouns from Task 1.
5 My hobby is .... I've got lots of books in my room.
6 We sometimes go .... at the weekend. I have my own tent.
7 James wins prizes for .... He's very good. Look at this picture.
8 I love .... when the music is fast.

[4]

Task 3
Match the sentence beginnings (9–15) with the endings (A–G).
9 Jake enjoys collecting ....
10 My brother sometimes plays ....
11 I sometimes watch ....
12 My dad always listens ....
13 I often go ....
14 My mum is very sporty and often plays ....
15 There's a new film and I want to go ....

A video games in his room for hours!
B a film with my family in the evening.
C football on Saturdays for her club.
D to the cinema to watch it.
E comics about superheroes.
F shopping with my friends at the weekend.
G to the radio in the garden.

[7]

Task 4
Choose the correct answer (A, B or C).
16 My sister often .... cakes and we eat them after dinner.
   A does   B draws   C bakes
17 I've got a baby brother and he loves watching .... on TV.
   A comics   B cartoons   C postcards
18 My mum always listens .... music when she's cooking.
   A to   B at   C on
19 Do you want to go on a .... this weekend?
   A shopping   B sleepover   C cinema
20 I think it's boring to .... books every evening.
   A read   B listen   C play
21 My dad is very .... at and sometimes wins competitions.
   A enjoy   B good   C like
22 Do you play .... with your family at the weekend?
   A films   B competitions C cards
23 I sometimes play the .... in a band at school.
   A guitar   B postcards   C radio
24 I love this comic. I think it's ....
   A not good   B like   C awesome
25 Do you often .... videos?
   A watch   B collect   C go

[10]

UNIT 1: LANGUAGE TEST B

GRAMMAR

Task 1
Complete the sentences with the present simple form of the verbs in brackets.

26 Eva and Tom usually .... (play) video games together after dinner.
27 My sister .... (not / want) to watch a film this evening. She's got a lot of homework.
28 Small children .... (often / enjoy) watching cartoons.
29 What music .... (you / like) to listen to?
30 .... (your dad / work) in town?
31 I .... (not / collect) football cards now. I collect comics.
32 Where .... (your best friend / live)?
33 My mum .... (not / bake) cakes very often.
34 My brother .... (watch) videos all the time.
35 .... (your friends / like) fishing in the river?

10

Task 2
Complete each sentence with *much* or *many*.

36 How .... comics have you got?
37 Do you spend .... time listening to music?
38 There isn't .... food in the fridge.
39 How .... video games has your brother got?
40 It's not .... fun to work all weekend.

5

Task 3
Put the words in the correct order to make sentences.

41 hot / is / in summer / always / It / .
....

42 never / on Saturday / go to school / we / .
....

43 goes swimming / Marie / after school / sometimes / .
....

44 doesn't / My dad / drive to work / often / .
....

45 early / I'm / for lessons / usually / .
....

10

Total: 50

UNIT 1: SKILLS TEST A

DICTATION

You will hear a recording about a person's hobbies. Listen and write what you hear.
You will hear the recording twice.

....

....

....

| 10 |

LISTENING

You will hear a girl, Annie, phoning a friend about a talent competition. You will hear the recording twice.

Task 1

Complete the information. Write one word, or a number, or a date, or a time.

Talent competition	
Place:	Bank College
Day:	(1) ....
Time it begins:	(2) ....
Who to report to:	Miss (3) ....
Phone number to apply:	(4) ....
Second prize:	(5) £ ....

| 15 |

Task 2

Complete the sentences.

6 Annie is calling with .... news.
7 The competition is for ....
8 It finishes at ....
9 Eva and Maria are .... in the competition.
10 The first prize is ....

| 5 |

Photocopiable © Pearson Education Limited 2018

UNIT 1: SKILLS TEST A

READING

Read the text and answer the questions.

My dad

My dad works in the centre of town and we live in the country. He's got a fantastic old car, but does he drive to work? No, he doesn't. Every day he goes by train. His car stays at home! He loves it! He spends hours every Saturday and Sunday with it. He cleans it, he repairs it. He even talks to it! We can't touch it. It's his main hobby and definitely his best friend!

My brother, Luke

Our house isn't very quiet in the evenings. My brother, Luke, enjoys playing the guitar in his room. He belongs to a school band. He thinks that's awesome. Sometimes they all come and play in his room! They're good and they often play at parties and earn some money. How much do they earn? A lot! Lucky Luke! He's got an electric guitar now. It's really loud, and my dad isn't happy about that.

My sister, Hannah

I like reading books and watching films, but my sister, Hannah, doesn't do normal hobbies like those! She loves spending money. She goes shopping every day! Sometimes she goes to the shops after college. Sometimes she buys things online. Her room is full of clothes, and she collects shoes – nearly a hundred pairs! Where does she get the money? She works on Saturdays at the supermarket. She earns a lot of money and then she spends it all in the week!

Task 1

Choose the correct answer (A, B or C).

Which person:

	Maya's dad	Luke	Hannah
11 has an expensive hobby?	A	B	C
12 gets money for doing a hobby?	A	B	C
13 only does a hobby at the weekends?	A	B	C
14 has a weekend job?	A	B	C
15 doesn't want help with a hobby?	A	B	C
16 has a hobby that is sometimes unpopular?	A	B	C
17 uses a computer to do a hobby?	A	B	C

[14]

Task 2

Answer the questions about the text.

18 What does Maya's dad like?

....

19 What does Luke like?

....

20 What does Hannah like?

....

[6]

Total: [50]

24 Photocopiable © Pearson Education Limited 2018

UNIT 1: SKILLS TEST B

DICTATION

You will hear a recording about a person's hobbies. You will hear the recording twice.

....

....

....

| 10 |

LISTENING

You will hear a girl, Annie, phoning a friend about a talent competition.
You will hear the recording twice.

Task 1

Complete the information. Write one word, or a number, or a date, or a time.

Talent competition

Place:	Bank College
Enter before:	**(1)** ....
Competition ends:	**(2)** ....
Competition will be in:	**(3)** ....
Give your name to:	Mr **(4)** ....
First prize:	**(5)** £...........................

| 15 |

Task 2

Complete the sentences.

6 Annie is calling with exciting ....
7 The competition is on ....
8 It starts at ....
9 Eva and Maria are not very .... at dancing.
10 The second prize is ....

| 5 |

Photocopiable © Pearson Education Limited 2018   25

UNIT 1: SKILLS TEST B

READING

Read the text and answer the questions.

My dad

In my friends' houses, their mums prepare the meals. It's different in our house. My dad's main hobby is cooking! He goes to classes after work and enjoys learning about meals from different countries. He can even bake cakes. So, he cooks for the family every evening – which is great for us all. Is he a good cook? Well, OK when he cooks easy meals! But he doesn't always remember to put sugar in the cakes. Ugh!

My mum

Every year we go to different countries on holiday. My mum loves learning languages so she can speak to the people. She knows French and Spanish. Now she's learning Italian. She goes to classes after work every Friday. She thinks they are brilliant. The teacher is my brother Ewan. Ewan teaches school children in the day and then he gives Italian classes in the evenings. Mum sometimes doesn't listen and talks when the teacher is saying something. Ewan often tells her to be quiet!

My sister, Alice

We've got two dogs, Polly and Silver, and for my sister, Alice, they're like children! She enjoys being with them, taking them for walks every morning and cleaning them every day. She also likes training them to walk and sit and be good. Polly and Silver are special dogs. They go in competitions and they often win prizes. Sometimes Alice takes them to France and Germany for competitions and I go with her. I'm learning to train the dogs too. It's fun, and the dogs love it!

Task 1

Choose the correct answer (A, B or C).

Which person:

	Eva's dad	Eva's mum	Alice
11 goes to other countries because of a hobby?	A	B	C
12 sometimes makes mistakes when doing a hobby?	A	B	C
13 learns something from a family member?	A	B	C
14 helps the family every day with his/her hobby?	A	B	C
15 wants to use a hobby while travelling?	A	B	C
16 is very good at a hobby?	A	B	C
17 sometimes doesn't listen?	A	B	C

14

Task 2

Answer the questions.

18 What does Eva's dad like?

....

19 What does Eva's mum like?

....

20 What does Alice like?

....

6

Total: 50

UNIT 2: LANGUAGE TEST A

VOCABULARY

Task 1
Complete the sentences with the correct words. Use the first letter to help you.

1 We've got a new television with a very big **s**............... . It's great!
2 My **w**............... isn't working, and my friends can't see me when we chat.
3 You can move around by using the arrow keys or the **m**............... .
4 The letter 'e' doesn't work on my **k**............... . It's really difficult to type anything!
5 The **s**............... on my computer aren't very good and I can't hear the music.
6 Please put some paper in the **p**............... .
7 I bought a new **d**............... **c**..............., so I can take photos on holiday.
8 I can hear your **m**............... **p**............... ringing. Is it in your bag?

[8]

Task 2
Complete the sentences with these words.

an email   click   download   have   music   visit

9 I want to send .... to my friend in the USA this evening.
10 We sometimes stream .... on the computer.
11 .... on the link in my email to go to the website.
12 I usually .... films from this website. I can watch them later.
13 On the train they .... free WiFi. It's good when I'm travelling to school.
14 Do you .... online with your friends every day?
15 Lots of people .... this website. It's very popular.

[7]

Task 3
Choose the correct answer (A, B or C).

16 I always use .... to listen to music on a train.
   A speakers   B headphones   C keyboard
17 My friend .... her own vlog and it's really interesting.
   A makes   B gives   C takes
18 I'm using a .... app to understand what this sentence is about.
   A download   B translator   C WiFi
19 After school I often .... my friend to meet at the café.
   A message   B chat   C speaker
20 Jacky is sitting in .... of me in class.
   A next   B behind   C front
21 My dad often takes his .... with him on holiday for work.
   A printer   B social media   C laptop
22 The internet café is next .... the bank.
   A of   B to   C at
23 Use your .... app to send Anna the information.
   A messaging   B game   C music
24 You need a .... when you chat online and want to see the other person's face.
   A stream   B webcam   C tablet
25 Go to our website and you can .... the music.
   A click   B visit   C download

[10]

Photocopiable © Pearson Education Limited 2018

UNIT 2: LANGUAGE TEST A

GRAMMAR

Task 1
Write the *-ing* forms of these verbs.
26 lie ....
27 type ....
28 chat ....
29 message ....
30 stream ....

[5]

Task 2
Complete the sentences with the present continuous form of the verbs in brackets.
31 .... (he / lie) on his bed in his room?
32 What .... (you / type) on your keyboard?
33 She .... (not / message) her friend.
34 I .... (stream) a great film online.
35 They .... (not / chat) at the moment.

[5]

Task 3
Complete the answers with the correct words.
36 A: Is Sarah working right now?
   B: No, she ....
37 A: Are your friends playing football?
   B: Yes, they ....
38 A: Are you doing your homework at the moment?
   B: No, I ....
39 A: Are Mike and Lucy watching a film?
   B: Yes, they ....
40 A: Is your brother practising his guitar now?
   B: Yes, he ....

[5]

Task 4
Complete the sentences with the present simple or continuous form of the verbs in brackets.
41 I .... next to my best friend in class today. (sit)
42 I .... films on TV because I usually stream them online. (not / watch)
43 What .... at the moment? Is he playing the guitar? (your brother / do)
44 I love this new messaging app! I .... it right now! (use)
45 .... to chat online this evening when I get home? (you / want)

[10]

Total: [50]

Name: _____

Class: _____

UNIT 2: LANGUAGE TEST B

VOCABULARY

Task 1

Complete the sentences with the correct words. Use the first letter to help you.

1 I always use a **w**………………… when I'm chatting online. My friends can see my face.
2 What's that music? Oh, it's your **m**………………… **p**…………………! Perhaps Mike is calling you.
3 My **k**………………… is old. You can't see the letters 'r' and 't' now!
4 I always wear special **h**………………… when I go running to listen to music.
5 Our school gives each student a **l**…………………. They work on them in class.
6 There's no more paper in the **p**………………….
7 I've got a **d**………………… **c**………………… for my brother's birthday. He likes taking photos.
8 My phone's got a very small **s**………………….
It's difficult to read messages!

[8]

Task 2

Complete the sentences with these words.

email   link   my friends   online   stream
video   website

9 We're making a ………………… in class. It's fun!
10 I often ………………… music on my tablet.
11 My mum visits this ………………… every day. It has all the latest news.
12 After school I message ………………… and we meet in the café.
13 My mum sometimes chats ………………… to her friends in France.
14 I'm sending this ………………… to all my friends to tell them what time to meet before the concert.
15 The teacher wants us to click on this ………………… to find the information.

[7]

Task 3

Choose the correct answer (A, B or C).

16 You can use the …… or the arrow keys to move the cursor.
   A tablet   **B** screen   **C** mouse
17 They …… free WiFi in the café.
   A make   **B** have   **C** are
18 My dad's car is the red one …… yours.
   A next   **B** between   **C** behind
19 I usually …… music to my phone and listen to it later.
   A download   **B** make   **C** play
20 In France I used my …… app to help me understand signs and menus.
   A maps   **B** messaging   **C** translator
21 The …… on my computer aren't very good and I can't hear the music.
   A speakers   **B** webcams   **C** mouse
22 The internet café is …… of the garage on the High Street.
   A opposite   **B** in front   **C** at
23 My friends and I chat on social …… all the time.
   A online   **B** apps   **C** media
24 I take my …… on trains because it's easy to carry.
   A tablet   **B** printer   **C** screen
25 What does that message on your …… mean?
   A screen   **B** mouse   **C** app

[10]

Photocopiable © Pearson Education Limited 2018

Name: _____
Class: _____

UNIT 2: LANGUAGE TEST B

GRAMMAR

Task 1

Write the *-ing* forms of these verbs.

26 give ....
27 send ....
28 sit ....
29 write ....
30 lie ....

☐ 5

Task 2

Complete the sentences with the present continuous form of the verbs in brackets.

31 .... (you / write) your essay?
32 The teacher .... (not / give) us a test today.
33 We .... (sit) in the classroom, but the teacher isn't here!
34 My mum isn't feeling well and .... (lie) down on the bed.
35 .... (this computer / send) the email or not?

☐ 5

Task 3

Complete the answers with the correct words.

36 A: Are the children playing in the garden?
  B: No, they ....
37 A: Is Katy working on her computer?
  B: Yes, she ....
38 A: Are you doing your homework at the moment?
  B: No, I ....
39 A: Are your parents watching TV right now?
  B: Yes, they ....
40 A: Are you waiting for Mark?
  B: Yes, I ....

☐ 5

Task 4

Complete the sentences with the present simple or continuous form of the verbs in brackets.

41 Do you often download music from a website? I .... to download some songs now, but it's very slow. (try)
42 My dad's a translator. He .... for a big communications company in the city. (work)
43 What .... ? I'd like to get those headphones, but I haven't got much money. (you / buy)
44 My mum .... today. She's on holiday. (not work)
45 Kate .... my laptop because her laptop is at home. (use)

☐ 10

Total: ☐ 50

30 Photocopiable © Pearson Education Limited 2018

Name: _____

Class: _____

UNIT 2: SKILLS TEST A

DICTATION

You will hear a recording about a mobile phone. Listen and write what you hear.
You will hear the recording twice.

....

....

....

| 10 |

LISTENING

Listen to five short conversations and answer the questions. You will hear the recording twice.

Task 1

Choose the correct picture (A, B or C).

1 When is computer club?

A B C

2 What is the prize for the winner of the competition?

A B C

3 Who is having a party?

4 Which app has the boy got?

A B C

5 What time can the boy talk to the girl on the phone?

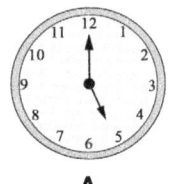  

A B C

A B C

| 15 |

Task 2

Complete the sentences.

6 The .... club is on Wednesday.
7 The next three people win .... in the competition.
8 The girl is in the café with ....
9 The girl likes to use the .... app.
10 The TV programme finishes at ....

| 5 |

Name: _____
Class: _____

UNIT 2: SKILLS TEST A

READING

Read the post and answer the questions.

Task 1

Write the correct answer in each gap. Write one word for each gap.

Are you looking for something to do at the weekend? **(11)** .... you want to help people? We've got the answer!

Teenagers know a lot **(12)** .... technology. We can email, message our friends, surf the internet and play video games. But some people don't know **(13)** .... to use computers. Can your gran or grandad get information from websites or chat online? Our group visits older people in **(14)** .... homes and we teach them computer skills. So, we are looking for teenagers **(15)** .... join us. We visit people in Langdown town centre and up to five kilometres outside Langdown. You don't earn any money, but we pay for your travel.

So, why **(16)** .... you waiting? It's great fun and we're helping a lot of people!

Emmy

This is a brilliant idea! My gran is seventy and she lives 200 km away from us. I'd really like to chat online with her. She's got a computer, but she isn't very good at using it! I hope there's a group like this near her.

Jack

Yes. I want to join. There's an old man opposite us and he never gets visitors. I'd like to help him. Sometimes older people don't have family near them. Then the computer's important.

Pippa

I belong to the group. It's very good. I visit three people in the town centre. They love learning and now they're very good. They can visit websites, download information. One man is writing a story with his computer!

---

[12]

Task 2

Choose the correct answer (A, B or C).

Which person:

	Emmy	Jack	Pippa
17 is already a member of the group?	A	B	C
18 would like to be a member of the group?	A	B	C
19 hopes there is another group in a different area?	A	B	C
20 wants to help someone who lives nearby?	A	B	C

[8]

Total: [50]

UNIT 2: SKILLS TEST B

DICTATION

You will hear a recording about a mobile phone. Listen and write what you hear.
You will hear the recording twice.

....

....

....

| 10 |

LISTENING

Listen to five short conversations and answer the questions. You will hear the recording twice.

Task 1

Choose the correct picture (A, B or C).

1 When is photo club?

4 Which app does the girl use every day?

2 What can three people win in the competition?

5 What time does the girl have dinner?

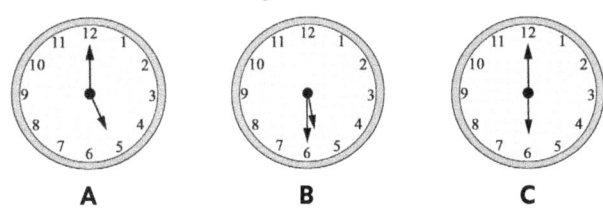

3 Who is the girl with at the moment?

| 15 |

Task 2

Complete the sentences.

6 The .... club is on Monday.
7 The first prize in the competition is a ....
8 It's ....'s birthday today.
9 The boy likes to use an app to check .... times.
10 The boy finishes dinner at ....

| 5 |

Photocopiable © Pearson Education Limited 2018   33

UNIT 2: SKILLS TEST B

READING

Read the post and answer the questions.

Task 1

Write the correct answer in each gap. Write one word for each gap.

Do you spend lots of evenings playing computer games? Perhaps you **(11)** .... getting bored and you want another interesting hobby? It's great to play games, but it's also great to make **(12)** .... ! Our club is for 13–18-year-olds and our members learn **(13)** .... create video games. We meet every Thursday evening after school. We ask expert games designers to come and talk to us. **(14)** .... teach us how to design great games.

Some technology teachers from school also come to help. Our club is free! So come on Thursday and you can have an amazing time.

Perhaps you want to design computer games in **(15)** .... future! It starts here! One member, Tim Parker, now works for a games company! Tell all **(16)** .... friends and visit our website now!

Gemma

This is a great idea. I love playing and talking about games. Thursdays are good for me. My friend Sasha wants me to join. She thinks it's a cool club. She says that the people are fun and the teachers help a lot. It's good to meet other people with the same interests.

Carl

I go to a games club in the town centre on Saturdays. It's OK. We play games and talk about computers. But I'd like to learn skills for making games. I think this club is cool and I'd like to join!

Lulu

I love this club. It's amazing. I want to design computer games for a career and now I know a lot of useful things. Tim Parker's new game is brilliant!

12

Task 2

Choose the correct answer (A, B or C).

Which person:

	Gemma	Carl	Lulu
17 is a member of the club?	A	B	C
18 knows a member of the group?	A	B	C
19 goes to a different club?	A	B	C
20 likes Tim's new game?	A	B	C

8

Total: 50

UNIT 3: LANGUAGE TEST A

VOCABULARY

Task 1
Put the letters in the correct order to make school subjects.

1 ybgiool ....
2 trosp ....
3 shspyci ....
4 toryshi ....
5 thcyrmehsi ....

[5]

Task 2
Complete the sentences with these words.

bookshelf   art   gym   board   pupil
timetable   geography

6 I painted a good picture in my .... lesson today.
7 My dad was a .... at my school twenty years ago!
8 Our teacher wrote the explanation on the ....
9 The teacher asked us to look at a map of Africa in my .... lesson this morning.
10 Most of our sports lessons are in the ....
11 The .... for Thursday is great – we've got lots of free lessons!
12 There are a lot of dictionaries on the .... in our classroom.

[7]

Task 3
Complete the sentences with the correct form of these verbs.

get   learn   wear   write

13 I .... a red and grey uniform to my Primary school.
14 I'm happy because I .... a good mark for my English essay yesterday.
15 My friends and I .... Spanish for a year when we were twelve.
16 The teacher .... some sentences on the board this morning and we copied them.

[8]

Task 4
Choose the correct answer (A, B or C).

17 In .... we learn about numbers.
   A geography   B art   C maths
18 My .... in the maths test was seventy-five percent.
   A note   B mark   C board
19 I stayed home all weekend and .... bored.
   A went   B got   C had
20 My dad sent a letter to the school ....
   A office   B gym   C lab
21 I've got a new football .... for school.
   A uniform   B pitch   C shirt

[5]

UNIT 3: LANGUAGE TEST A

GRAMMAR

Task 1
Write the past simple form of the irregular verbs.
22 buy ....
23 eat ....
24 know ....
25 read ....
26 win ....

[5]

Task 2
Complete the sentences with the past simple form of the verbs in brackets.
27 I .... (meet) members of my art club last Friday.
28 Jacky .... (make) some sandwiches for the picnic last weekend.
29 There .... (be) a lot of people – at the school play last night.
30 I .... (see) my cousin – at the football match on Sunday.
31 My dad .... (walk) to work this morning.

[5]

Task 3
Write the sentences in the negative.
32 Amanda and I took the train to school this morning.

....

33 My mum heard the news on the radio this morning.

....

34 Our teacher spoke to us in English today.

....

35 I did my homework today.

....

36 We had a long lunch break yesterday.

....

[5]

Task 4
Complete the sentences with the correct past simple form of the verbs in brackets.
37 A: ....
   (you / find / your homework) your homework last night?
   B: No, I didn't.
38 A: ....
   (Where / Tom / go) after school today?
   B: To the café.
39 A: ....
   (How long / you / stay) at Kerry's party on Friday?
   B: Only an hour.
40 A: ....
   (Mark / message / you) about plans for the weekend?
   B: Yes, he did.
41 A: Were your parents at home yesterday evening?
   B: No, ...
   (they / not / be)

[10]

Total: [50]

GOLD experience 2ND EDITION A2 Key for Schools

UNIT 3: LANGUAGE TEST B

VOCABULARY

Task 1
Put the letters in the correct order to make school subjects.

1 pryohegga ....
2 stahm ....
3 tra ....
4 strop ....
5 goboyli ....

[5]

Task 2
Complete the sentences with these words.

chemistry   desks   history   marks
note   office   ruler

6 We have all our .... lessons in the science lab.
7 Here's a .... from Harry about the room change this afternoon.
8 Kathy went to the school .... to speak to the secretary about her holiday.
9 .... is my favourite subject because there are stories about kings and queens.
10 The teacher asked us to sit down and put our books on our ....
11 What were your .... in the tests last week?
12 I can never draw a line without a .... !

[7]

Task 3
Complete the sentences with the correct form of these verbs.

get   have   write

13 The teacher was angry because we all .... bad marks in the French test.
14 What time do you usually .... home after school?
15 We .... a lot of homework last weekend.
16 I .... the words in my notebook and learned them for homework.

[8]

Task 4
Choose the correct answer (A, B or C).

17 I usually .... my homework in my bedroom.
  A make   B have   C do
18 Six .... in my class weren't at school yesterday because they were ill.
  A marks   B rulers   C pupils
19 I don't like the new .... because there's lots of maths on Friday!
  A board   B timetable   C ruler
20 My English friend .... a uniform to school.
  A has   B wears   C gets
21 We learn about how things move and how the world works in ....
  A physics   B chemistry   C history

[5]

Photocopiable © Pearson Education Limited 2018   37

GOLD experience 2ND EDITION A2

UNIT 3: LANGUAGE TEST B

GRAMMAR

Task 1
Write the past simple form of the irregular verbs.

22 come ....
23 go ....
24 have ....
25 meet ....
26 see ....

[ ] 5

Task 2
Complete the sentences with the past simple form of the verbs in brackets.

27 We .... (get) to school late this morning.
28 I .... (find) my notebook under my bed.
29 The teacher .... (hear) my phone in the lesson.
30 My dad .... (speak) French when he was young.
31 I .... (spend) my lunchbreak in the library today.

[ ] 5

Task 3
Write the sentences in the negative.

32 I wore a uniform at my last school.

....

33 We saw that film at the cinema last month.

....

34 My brother was in the school office this morning.

....

35 The teacher gave us a lot of homework today.

....

36 The dictionaries were on the bookshelf.

....

[ ] 5

Task 4
Complete the sentences with the correct past simple form of the verbs in brackets.

37 A: ....
(Where / you / do) your homework yesterday?
B: In the library.

38 A: Did you meet Jack after school?
B: No, I ....
(I / not)

39 A: ....
(Molly / win) the competition?
B: Yes, she did.

40 A: ....
(Where / you / be) on Saturday?
B: I was with my friend.

41 A: ....
(What mark / Sam / get) in his exam last week?
B: Eighty-five percent!

[ ] 10

Total: [ ] 50

GOLD experience
2ND EDITION A2 Key for Schools

Name:
Class:

UNIT 3: SKILLS TEST A

DICTATION

You will hear a recording about schools. Listen and write what you hear. You will hear the recording twice.

....

....

....

[10]

LISTENING

You will hear Jenna talking to her friend, Nick, about their parents' schools.
You will hear the recording twice.

Task 1

Choose the correct answer (A, B or C).

1 Jenna's mum was at school with ....
 A sixty-five pupils **B** 200 pupils **C** 500 pupils
2 Her dad didn't go to school on ....
 A Mondays **B** Wednesdays **C** Fridays
3 In class Nick likes ....
 A to change groups **B** to sit at desks **C** to be next to his friend
4 What homework has Nick got for the weekend?
 A all subjects **B** English and maths **C** English
5 Nick went to his first school in ....
 A England **B** the USA **C** Japan

[15]

Task 2

Answer the questions.

6 Where did the girl's parents go to school?

....

7 What days did they go to school?

....

8 What were their classrooms like?

....

9 What homework did they get?

....

10 Why did the boy's parents have different school experiences?

....

[5]

GOLD experience 2ND EDITION — A2 Key for Schools

Name:

Class:

UNIT 3: SKILLS TEST A

READING

Read the text and answer the questions.

Everyone knows that it's often difficult for students to concentrate on their work at school. We asked our readers for some answers.

Alex

Yes – it's a big problem! Last year it was very hard. We had a lot of tests at school and the teachers gave us hours of homework. I worked until 10.30 every night. I didn't have time to go swimming or watch TV. My friends did the same. We didn't get much sleep because we got up at 6.30 in the morning to go to school. We were all very tired in the mornings. I often wanted to stay in bed and not go to school!

One day, five students went to sleep during maths! Our teacher was worried, and she had an idea. She and the other teachers talked about the problem. They suggested a different start time for school – 9.00 and not 8.00. We finished at the usual time, but we had a short lunch and short break times.

At first, we weren't sure about the idea. We liked long break times with our friends. But after a week everyone agreed. It was a good change! We weren't tired, and we could study. The idea was to have the change for only two months until our exams and then go back to the old times. But after two months, they decided to keep the new start time.

We're all happy now because we can stay in bed. The teachers are happy because we don't go to sleep in their classes!

Task 1

Choose the correct answer (A, B or C).

11 Why did Alex and his friends go to bed late?
  A They watched a lot of TV.
  B They did a lot of school work.
  C They did sports.

12 When did a teacher understand there was a problem?
  A Pupils didn't come to classes.
  B Pupils were late for school.
  C Pupils slept in class.

13 What changes did the school make?
  A the time the school day began
  B the number of breaks during the school day
  C the time the school day ended

14 The pupils didn't like the changes in the beginning because
  A they wanted more time with their friends.
  B they had problems getting to school.
  C they liked finishing early.

15 What time do pupils at Alex's school start lessons now?
  A 8.00
  B 9.00
  C 10.30

Task 2

Answer the questions.

16 Why did Alex and his friends have a lot of homework?
....

17 Who had an idea to solve the problem?
....

18 Why was this a good idea?
....

19 How long did the school first want the changes to last?
....

20 How do the teachers feel now and why?
....

10

Total: 50

10

GOLD experience 2ND EDITION A2 Key for Schools

UNIT 3: SKILLS TEST B

DICTATION

You will hear a recording about schools. Listen and write what you hear. You will hear the recording twice.

....

....

....

| 10 |

LISTENING

You will hear Jenna talking to her friend, Nick, about their parents' schools.
You will hear the recording twice.

Task 1

Choose the correct answer (A, B or C).

1 Jenna's dad went to school with ....
   A sixty-five pupils   B 200 pupils   C 500 pupils
2 How many days did her mum go to school?
   A four   B five   C six
3 Jenna's parents ....
   A sat in groups   B sat in a line   C moved desks into circles
4 What homework does Nick's class have for the weekend?
   A English   B English and maths   C maths
5 Nick's dad went to school in ....
   A England   B the USA   C Japan

| 15 |

Task 2

Answer the questions.

6 Where did the girl's parents go to school?
....
7 What days did they go to school?
....
8 What were their classrooms like?
....
9 What homework did they get?
....
10 Why did the boy's parents have different school experiences?
....

| 5 |

GOLD experience 2ND EDITION A2 Key for Schools

UNIT 3: SKILLS TEST B

READING

Read the text and answer the questions.

Everyone knows that it is often difficult for students to concentrate at school. We asked our readers for some answers.

Harry

Yes – it's really difficult to study at school when you're tired. We get a lot of homework every night. Sometimes I watch TV after doing my work and then I go to bed very late. I like playing online games with friends in different countries, but I haven't got time.

About a year ago, it was very bad. Some pupils in my class were very tired and went to sleep in class! So, the school decided to make some changes. At my cousin's school they changed the start time – 9.00 and not 8.00 – and finished the school day later. But at our school they did something different. They changed our start time to from 8.00 to 9.00 too, but we finished at the usual time. We had a short lunch break, and they organised Saturday morning lessons! They were not popular!

My friends were angry because they couldn't have swimming or tennis lessons, and other pupils liked to go away for weekends. The lessons continued on Saturday mornings for two months, but then they stopped. Many parents wrote letters to the school to complain. Also, a lot of pupils didn't go to the lessons! The teachers organised a big meeting for all the pupils and we talked about the problem.

Now we start at 9.00, but we finish later, like at my cousin's school. It's fine. We're all happy because we can stay in bed for another hour and Saturdays are free. The teachers are happy because we don't go to sleep in their classes!

Task 1

Choose the correct answer (A, B or C).

11 Why does Harry sometimes go to sleep late?
 A he chats to friends online
 B he plays games on his computer
 C he watches TV

12 What changes did Harry's school first make?
 A They started and finished later than usual.
 B They did lessons at the weekend.
 C They did homework at lunchtime.

13 Some pupils didn't like the changes because they wanted to
 A do sports.
 B stay in bed.
 C go out with friends.

14 How did the school decide the next change?
 A They asked the parents.
 B They asked the pupils.
 C They asked the teachers.

15 What happens at Harry's school now?
 A They use the old school times.
 B They work on Saturdays.
 C They start late and finish late.

Task 2

Answer the questions.

16 What was the problem for Harry and his friends?
....

17 What did the school do about the problem, at first?
....

18 How did the pupils feel?
....

19 What did the school do next about the problem?
....

20 How does Harry feel now?
....

10

Total: 50

10

GOLD experience 2ND EDITION — A2 Key for Schools

UNIT 4: LANGUAGE TEST A

VOCABULARY

Task 1
Complete the words for types of money.
1 £5 = five p _ _ _ _ s
2 $2 = two d _ _ _ _ _ s
3 €1 = one e _ _ _
4 10p = ten p _ _ _ _
5 50¢ = fifty c _ _ _ s

[5]

Task 2
Complete the sentences with these words.

bargain   cash   closed   cost   receipt
sale   save   sell   spend   try

6 There was a .... at the shop and these jeans weren't very expensive.
7 The café was .... and we couldn't get a sandwich.
8 Did you .... all the money you took on holiday?
9 Keep the .... and then you can change the shoes if you want.
10 I didn't have any .... so I paid by card.
11 I can .... on the dress, but I think it's the wrong size.
12 This laptop was a .... I only paid £50 for it!
13 How much did the meal .... ?
14 My brother wants to .... some money this month so he can go on holiday in the summer.
15 I like your dad's new car. Did he .... his old, blue one?

[10]

Task 3
Complete the sentences with the correct places. Use the first letter to help you.
16 I found some interesting books in the l.................... .
17 They sell unusual fruit in the m.................... .
18 The band played a concert at the t.................... in the town centre.
19 You can buy lots of different things in a d.................... s.................... .
20 I went to the t.................... i.................... office to get a list of good hotels.

[5]

Task 4
Choose the correct answer (A, B or C).

Last weekend I went to a new (21) .... shop to buy some trainers with my friend. I tried (22) .... lots of pairs, but I couldn't find one in the right (23) .... So we went to the new sports shop. It was amazing! They had gym machines in there. People could do some exercise and check how the trainers felt! What a great idea. And the (24) .... was really good. They only (25) .... £30.00. What a bargain!

21 A book   B clothes   C music
22 A in   B at   C on
23 A receipt   B sale   C size
24 A price   B bargain   C cash
25 A sell   B cost   C buy

[5]

Photocopiable © Pearson Education Limited 2018

GOLD experience 2ND EDITION — A2 Key for Schools

UNIT 4: LANGUAGE TEST A

GRAMMAR

Task 1
Write the comparative form of the adjectives.

26 pretty ....
27 new ....
28 good ....
29 high ....
30 difficult ....
31 thin ....
32 far ....
33 happy ....
34 important ....
35 small ....

[ ] 5

Task 2
Complete the sentences with the comparative form of these adjectives.

bad   busy   exciting   near   sunny

36 The second film is .... than the first one was. I loved it!
37 My dad is working on the computer again. He's .... than he was last month.
38 My chemistry marks are .... than yours. I didn't work hard enough for the test.
39 It was .... in Spain than it is in the UK. In the UK it rains too much.
40 Let's walk to my house. It's .... than yours.

[ ] 5

Task 3
Complete the sentences with the comparative or superlative form of the adjectives in brackets.

41 Jacky got .... marks in the class. He's top of the class! (good)
42 It's .... to carry cards than cash. (easy)
43 Exercise 3 is .... one on the page. I can't do it. (difficult)
44 Eva is .... girl I know. She's always smiling. (happy)
45 Sometimes small tablets are .... than big ones. (expensive)

[ ] 5

Task 4
Complete the text. Write one or two words for each gap.

Everyone has got a hobby or an interest and some are **(46)** .... expensive than others. But my sister's hobby is perhaps **(47)** .... expensive hobby you can have – it's shopping! She loves sales. When she sees something that is cheaper **(48)** .... usual, she buys it! She can't walk past a shop with a sales sign! And my best friend **(49)** .... worse than my sister! She's got **(50)** .... biggest shopping bag you can imagine. And on Saturdays, it's always full.

[ ] 10

Total: [ ] 50

UNIT 4: LANGUAGE TEST B

VOCABULARY

Task 1
Complete the words for different places.

1 A place where you can buy lots of different food:
   s _ _ _ _ _ _ _ _ _ _
2 a place where you can watch plays and concerts:
   t _ _ _ _ _ _
3 a place where you can find where to visit in a town:
   t _ _ _ _ _ _ information
4 a place where you can buy things outside: m _ _ _ _ _
5 A big shop where you can buy different types of things like clothes, lights, beds etc. d _ _ _ _ _ _ _ _ _ store

[5]

Task 2
Complete the sentences with these words.

| bargain | card | open | pay | price | receipt |
| save | sale | spent | tried | | |

6 How much did you .... for your new smart phone?
7 I .... on ten pairs of shoes, but I didn't like any of them!
8 The sports shop is .... now, so I can buy some new trainers.
9 I didn't keep the .... for this T-shirt, so I can't change it.
10 My sister .... too much money when she was in London!
11 The computer shop is having a .... and I want to buy a cheap tablet.
12 I work in a supermarket on Saturdays because I want to .... some money for a new computer.
13 The machine didn't accept my .... so I used cash.
14 The .... of the watch was less than I thought and I bought it for mum's birthday.
15 These sunglasses were a .... They were only $7!

[10]

Task 3
Complete the sentences with the correct places. Use the first letter to help you.

16 I'm going to the l............ because I want to borrow some books.
17 Let's go through the p............ and sit on the grass to eat our sandwiches.
18 We had a school trip to a m............ last week and looked at some old pictures.
19 My friends and I often go to the swimming p............ in the sports centre. It's great fun!
20 How much are the tickets for the new play at the t............ ?

[5]

Task 4
Choose the correct answer (A, B or C).

On Saturdays I work in a (21) .... People love shopping outside and it's always busy. I help my uncle. He (22) .... fruit and vegetables. It's great fun! People usually pay with (23) .... so I don't worry about card machines! At the end of the day the fruit is cheaper than in the morning and people can get a lot of (24) .... Sometimes I buy clothes in my lunch break. You can't (25) .... them on, but I know the sellers so I can always take them back if the size isn't right!

21 A supermarket   B sports shop   C market
22 A pays   B sells   C spends
23 A pence   B cash   C receipts
24 A bargains   B sales   C costs
25 A wear   B try   C look

[5]

GOLD experience 2ND EDITION A2

UNIT 4: LANGUAGE TEST B

GRAMMAR

Task 1
Write the comparative form of the adjectives.
26 sad ....
27 interesting ....
28 bad ....
29 near ....
30 sunny ....
31 low ....
32 exciting ....
33 busy ....
34 old ....
35 fat ....

Task 2
Complete the sentences with the comparative form of these adjectives.

| difficult   far   happy   high   important |

36 It's .... to do my English homework than my Maths homework because we've got English tomorrow.
37 My marks are .... than my sister's and she isn't pleased!
38 My new school is .... from my house than my old one so I take the bus.
39 Exercise 3 is .... than exercise 1 and I can't do it.
40 People are .... when the sun shines than when it's cold and rainy.

Task 3
Complete the sentences with the comparative or superlative form of the adjectives in brackets.
41 Mark is .... pupil in the class. He's never at school! (bad)
42 The clothes are .... in the new clothes shop than in the old one. (cheap)
43 Jack's picture of his dog is .... picture on his website. (funny)
44 I think Carl's article was .... one in the school newsletter. (interesting)
45 My dad says it's .... to save money than to spend it! (good)

Task 4
Complete the text. Write one or two words for each gap.

Are things more expensive online **(46)** .... in real shops? I don't think so, but I think people buy **(47)** .... things when they're online than when they are in a shop. **(48)** .... worst thing about online shopping is that it's very easy to do! For some people leaving a shopping website is **(49)** .... difficult thing in the world! For me, it's **(50)** .... interesting to go round shops and look at things than to look at things on a screen.

Total: 50

GOLD experience
2ND EDITION — A2 Key for Schools

Name: _____

Class: _____

UNIT 4: SKILLS TEST A

DICTATION

You will hear a recording about using money. Listen and write what you hear. You will hear the recording twice.

....

....

....

[ ] 10

LISTENING

Listen to five conversations and answer the questions. You will hear the recording twice.

Task 1

Choose the correct answer (A, B or C).

1. You will hear two friends talking about a new shopping centre. What does the girl like about it?
   - A It's near her home.
   - B It's got some nice gardens.
   - C It's got a lot of shops.

2. You will hear two friends talking about an online sale. Why didn't the boy buy a jacket?
   - A He didn't have the money.
   - B He couldn't get online.
   - C He didn't have the right information.

3. You will hear a boy talking about a birthday present. What is he going to buy?
   - A some speakers
   - B some headphones
   - C some CDs

4. You will hear two friends talking about some sunglasses. How much did the girl pay for them?
   - A 15 euros
   - B 50 euros
   - C 150 euros

5. You will hear two friends talking about the girl's Saturday job. Why does she like it?
   - A she can save money
   - B she finishes early
   - C she has polite customers

[ ] 15

Task 2

Complete the sentences with words from the conversations.

6. In the gardens, the girl ate some ....
7. The boy didn't know his ....
8. The boy is in the ....
9. The boy paid .... euros for his sunglasses.
10. The girl finishes work at ....

[ ] 5

Photocopiable © Pearson Education Limited 2018

GOLD experience
2ND EDITION — A2 Key for Schools

Name: _____

Class: _____

UNIT 4: SKILLS TEST A

READING

Read the text and answer the questions.

Task 1
Read the first part of the article. For each question write the correct answer. Write one word for each gap.

> OK, so you want some different computer games, **(11)** .... you haven't got enough money. This is because you spent it all when you went shopping **(12)** .... week. And you made a mistake. In the market, you bought a new T-shirt. You tried it on **(13)** .... home, but the T-shirt looked terrible! Yellow is **not** your colour. What can you do? You can't change **(14)** .... because you paid **(15)** .... it in cash, and you didn't keep the receipt. Now, all you can do is save money and wait **(16)** .... buy the computer game later. Or, you can exchange your T-shirt for a game.
>
> Exchanging, or 'swapping' things is becoming very popular. You can swap with your friends, your family, your classmates, and there are swapping websites too. It's good because you give away something that you don't want, and you get something that you do. Also – we put fewer things in the rubbish – and that's good for the environment!
>
> We don't always swap **things**. Imagine – your classmate has got some video games. He's also got a problem with his computer. You are good at repairing computers. You fix his computer, he gives you the games. Perfect!
>
> Swapping isn't a new way to get things. It was the first way, thousands of years ago. Then it was called 'bartering' and people exchanged food and warm clothes. Later, some people's job was travelling round the world to 'barter' different things in different countries. Today, we can do it from our laptops. So – who would like a nice orange jacket with green flowers on it?

[ ] 12

Task 2
Read the whole article. Decide if the questions are true (T) or false (F).

17 The writer loves her T-shirt.   ....
18 Swapping stops a lot of rubbish.   ....
19 People can swap skills for things.   ....
20 Swapping started when the internet began. ....

[ ] 8

Total: [ ] 50

GOLD experience 2ND EDITION — A2 Key for Schools

Name: _____

Class: _____

UNIT 4: SKILLS TEST B

DICTATION

You will hear a recording about using money. Listen and write what you hear. You will hear the recording twice.

....

....

....

| 10 |

LISTENING

Listen to five conversations and answer the questions. You will hear the recording twice.

Task 1

Choose the correct answer (A, B or C).

1 You will hear two friends talking about a new shopping centre. How did the girl get to the shopping centre?
 A on foot
 B by bus
 C by car

2 You will hear two friends talking about a sale. How did the boy want to buy the jacket?
 A on the phone
 B in a clothes shop
 C online

3 You will hear a boy talking about a birthday present. What did his dad get for his last birthday?
 A some CDs
 B some speakers
 C some headphones

4 You will hear two friends talking about some sunglasses. How much did the boy pay for them?
 A 15 euros
 B 50 euros
 C 150 euros

5 You will hear two friends talking about the girl's Saturday job. What does the girl have problems with?
 A the times
 B the clothes
 C the money

| 15 |

Task 2

Complete the sentences with words from the conversations.

6 The girl likes the .... at the shopping centre.
7 The sale lasted for .... hours.
8 The boy is thinking about buying .... for his father.
9 The girl paid for the sunglasses by ....
10 The girl starts work at .... o'clock in the morning.

| 5 |

GOLD experience 2ND EDITION A2

UNIT 4: SKILLS TEST B

READING

Read the text and answer the questions.

Task 1

Read the first part of the article. For each question write the correct answer. Write one word for each gap.

Right, so you want to buy **(11)** .... new computer games, but you spent all your money on clothes a few days **(12)** .... And, you didn't try on the T-shirt **(13)** .... the shop and it isn't the right size. **(14)** .... shop won't change the T-shirt because **(15)** .... was in a sale. What can you do? You can give the T-shirt **(16)** .... a friend. Then you can save more money and buy the games later on. Or you can use your T-shirt to get a new game right now!

Exchanging, or 'swapping' things is becoming very popular. You can swap with your friends, your family, your classmates, and there are swapping websites too. It's good because you give away something that you don't want, and you get something that you do. Also, we put fewer things in the rubbish – and that's good for the environment!

We don't always swap **things**. We can do actions instead. Imagine – your classmate has got some video games. He's also got a problem with his computer. You are good at repairing computers. You fix his computer, he gives you the games. Perfect!

Swapping isn't a new way to get things. It was the first way, thousands of years ago. Then it was called 'bartering' and people exchanged food and warm clothes. Later, some people's job was travelling round the world to 'barter' different things in different countries. Today we can do it from our laptops. So – who would like a nice orange jacket with green flowers on it?

12

Task 2

Read the whole article. Decide if the questions are true (T) or false (F).

17 You can get something you need without money.   ....
18 Most people don't like swapping things.   ....
19 We can swap skills for things.   ....
20 Swapping things only started recently.   ....

8

Total: 50

GOLD experience 2ND EDITION A2 Key for Schools

Name: _____

Class: _____

UNIT 5: LANGUAGE TEST A

VOCABULARY

Task 1
Complete the sentences with these words. There are two extra words.

___
actor   classical   comedy   electricity   festival   guitarist
magician   musician   sci-fi   sign   talent   theatre
___

1 We can't watch TV in our house in the mountains because there is no ………………… there.
2 You can't go in there – the ………………… on the door says *No entry*.
3 I enjoy both rock music and going to ………………… concerts.
4 ………………… movies are usually about life in the future.
5 I heard some great singers at a music ………………… last weekend.
6 A brilliant group of dancers won last night's ………………… show on TV.
7 In my favourite band there are a drummer, a ………………… and two singers.
8 I have no idea how the ………………… managed to get a rabbit out of that hat. It was an amazing trick.
9 Our class is going to see a play at the ………………… in our town this evening.
10 The film was a …………………, but I didn't think it was funny. I didn't laugh once!

[10]

Task 2
Choose the correct words to complete the sentences.

11 I don't like scary movies – I prefer **horror** / **romantic** films.
12 My painting of a dancer is going to be in the school art **animation** / **exhibition**.
13 I watched a very interesting **documentary** / **concert** about dolphins on TV last night.
14 Can you play a **musical instrument** / **rock**?
15 We sat outside, because it was an **open-air** / **exhibition** theatre.
16 Let's get a **seat** / **show** in the front row if we can.
17 This picture is by Picasso, my favourite **artist** / **comedian**.
18 What was your favourite **show** / **act** in the concert?
19 Do you enjoy watching **talent** / **action** films, with lots of fighting and car chases?
20 I like George Clooney. He is one of my favourite **actors** / **actresses**.

[10]

Task 3
Choose the correct answer (A, B or C).

21 …… films make you laugh.
   A Boring   B Funny   C Kind
22 It was a very …… film. I didn't understand it at all.
   A strange   B awesome   C kind
23 I loved the film. I thought it was …… !
   A terrible   B boring   C excellent
24 I liked the …… . She was very funny.
   A dancer   B comedian   C comedy
25 He can't …… . I don't like films with him in it.
   A actor   B actress   C act

[5]

UNIT 5: LANGUAGE TEST A

GRAMMAR

Task 1
Complete the sentences with the past continuous form of the verbs in brackets.

26 What film .... when I called you? (you / watching)
27 I .... to music. (listen)
28 My parents .... in the garden. (work)
29 The sun .... (shine)
30 My friends .... me yesterday. (visit)
31 We .... together. (study)
32 Then we .... a song for the school concert. (practise)
33 Why .... for me? (you / wait)

Task 2
Write the sentences in the negative.

34 I was playing the guitar all evening.

35 We were watching a horror film.

36 You were singing very well.

37 The girls were doing a magic trick.

38 The girl was going to a talent show.

Task 3
Make sentences with the past simple and the past continuous.

39 I / watch / a movie / when / you / text / me / .

40 she / sleep / when / thief / come in / .

41 my phone / ring / when / I / sit / on the bus / .

42 Jack / do / his homework / when / his friends / arrive / ?

43 we / see / some great T-shirts / when / we / walk / in town yesterday / .

44 the children / not play / football / when / the rain / start / .

GOLD experience 2ND EDITION — A2 Key for Schools

Name: _____
Class: _____

UNIT 5: LANGUAGE TEST B

VOCABULARY

Task 1

Complete the sentences with these words. There are two extra words.

actor   comedy   classical   electricity
exhibition   festival   guitarist   magician
musician   sci-fi   talent   theatre

1 Do you prefer .... music or pop music?
2 My favourite .... has the main part in a play on TV this evening.
3 My sister won first prize when she sang a song in a .... show last year.
4 I'd love to go to a .... festival and listen to lots of different bands.
5 I don't like .... movies – I prefer films about real life.
6 I want to go to the museum. They have an interesting art .... at the moment.
7 A ... above the door showed where the exit was.
8 My brother is a good .... – he can play the piano and the guitar very well.
9 Would you prefer to watch a sad film or a .... this evening?
10 We watched a great play at an open-air .... last night.

[10]

Task 2

Choose the correct words to complete the sentences.

11 I love scary movies, especially **horror / romantic** films.
12 Have you got anything in the school art **animation / exhibition** this year?
13 My brother is playing the guitar in a **documentary / concert** at school next week.
14 I'd love to play a musical **instrument / rock** well.
15 There is a music **exhibition / festival** in my town every summer.
16 Is the **seat/show** next to you free?
17 My mother is a very good **artist / comedian** – she paints lovely pictures.
18 Are you going to the talent **show / act** at school on Saturday?
19 **Documentary / Action** films are usually very exciting stories, with lots of things happening.
20 The word **actor / actress** can be used for a man or a woman.

[10]

Task 3

Choose the correct answer (A, B or C).

21 Nobody enjoys ...... films.
   A boring   B funny   C awesome
22 ...... films are usually about a love story.
   A Strange   B Scary   C Romantic
23 I didn't enjoy the film – I thought it was ...... !
   A terrible   B great   C excellent
24 ...... films don't usually have real people in them.
   A Action   B Animated C Awesome
25 I love films that are ...... stories about real people.
   A terrible   B sci-fi   C true

[5]

UNIT 5: LANGUAGE TEST B

GRAMMAR

Task 1

Complete the sentences with the past continuous form of the verbs in brackets.

26 What .... when I rang you? (you / do)
27 I .... TV. (watch)
28 My parents .... about a new film. (talk)
29 My brother .... some emails. (write)
30 We .... in the living room. (sit)
31 It .... all day yesterday. (rain)
32 Where .... when I saw him yesterday? (your brother / go)
33 He .... in the library yesterday. (work)

Task 2

Write the sentences in the negative.

34 I was dancing all evening.

35 We were listening to classical music.

36 You were laughing at the comedian's stories.

37 The boys were playing the piano very well.

38 The magician was doing a very difficult trick.

Task 3

Make sentences with the past simple and the past continuous.

39 we / wait / in the café / when our friend / come in / .

40 I / see / a famous singer / when / I / buy / a pair of new shoes yesterday / .

41 Grandma / fall / asleep / when we / watch / the news last night / .

42 I / not sleep / when you / phone / me / .

43 my sisters / play / in the garden / when you / call / .

44 you / listen / to the radio / when you / hear / the news / ?

GOLD experience
2ND EDITION — A2 Key for Schools

Name: _____
Class: _____

UNIT 5: SKILLS TEST A

DICTATION

You will hear a recording about watching a film. Listen and write what you hear. You will hear the recording twice.

....

....

....

[10]

LISTENING

Listen to five short conversations. You will hear the recording twice.

Task 1
Look at the pictures. Choose the correct answer (A, B or C).

1 How much was the girl's cinema ticket? 
   A £3.25   B £4.50   C £7.75

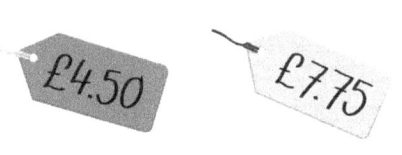

2 What time does the concert start?
   A    B    C 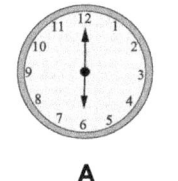

3 What did Nick buy at the festival?
   A    B 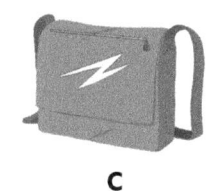   C 

4 Where did Fatima go yesterday? 
   A   B    C

5 What time did the talent show finish?
   A 9:50   B 10:00   C 10:10

[15]

Task 2
Complete the sentences.

6 The boy's ticket cost £ ....
7 The boy and girl want to meet at the ....
8 Nick went to a festival on ....
9 The girl's .... had some pictures at an exhibition.
10 Josh's .... picked him up.

[5]

Photocopiable © Pearson Education Limited 2018

GOLD experience 2ND EDITION   A2 Key for Schools

Name: _____

Class: _____

UNIT 5: SKILLS TEST A

READING

Read the text and answer the questions.

We asked three teenage reporters in London to tell us about an interesting cinema they have been to.

Emma

On my friend's birthday last week, her mum took us to an amazing cinema. We sat in the open air on the top of a big building. There were fantastic views over London. We weren't sitting in ordinary seats. Everyone had a deck chair, the kind of chair you usually see on a beach or on a ship! They were surprisingly comfortable! There was a huge screen in front of us. We watched an old film called *Casablanca*. It was very romantic and I loved it.

Dan

A couple of months ago I went with my cousin to something called the Secret Cinema. You buy tickets and then they email you to say where you will watch the film. We saw *Blade Runner*, a sci-fi movie, in a large old building that was once a factory. Everyone in the audience had to dress like a character from the film and some of the actors were there too. After the film, there was a party and I spoke to one of the main actors. He was really friendly!

Miranda

Yesterday, our whole class went to the cinema. We saw *Romeo and Juliet*, a film of the Shakespeare play which we're studying this year. The film was a bit too long for me, but I enjoyed it after the film when there was half an hour of questions and answers with one of the costume designers. The cinema where we were is not a business. All the money it makes goes to a social project in South Africa.

Task 1

Choose the correct answer (A, B or C).

Which person:

		Emma	Dan	Miranda
11	talked to someone who was in the film?	A	B	C
12	saw a film outside?	A	B	C
13	watched a film that was useful for their school work?	A	B	C
14	enjoyed watching a love story?	A	B	C
15	went to the film with one of their relatives?	A	B	C
16	did something useful for another country by watching a film?	A	B	C
17	wore special clothes when they went to the film?	A	B	C

14

Task 2

Answer the questions.

18 Why does Emma mention the seats at the cinema she went to?

....

19 Why do you think the Secret Cinema has this name?

....

20 What did Miranda not like about the experience?

....

6

Total: 50

GOLD experience
2ND EDITION — A2 Key for Schools

Name: _____

Class: _____

UNIT 5: SKILLS TEST B

DICTATION

You will hear a recording about watching a film. Listen and write what you hear.
You will hear the recording twice.

....

....

....

| 10 |

LISTENING

Listen to five short conversations. You will hear the recording twice.

Task 1

Look at the pictures. Choose the correct answer (A, B or C).

1 How much was the boy's cinema ticket? 
   A £3.25   B £4.50   C £7.75

2 What time are they going to meet? 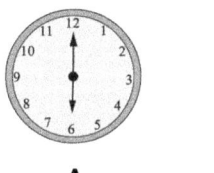
   A    B    C

3 What did the girl buy at the festival? 
   A (cap)   B (t-shirt)   C (bag)

4 Where did Andy go yesterday? 
   A    B    C

5 What time did the last bus leave?
   A 9:50   B 10:00   C 10:10

| 15 |

Task 2

Complete the sentences.

6 The girl's ticket cost £ ....
7 The boy and girl want to go to a ....
8 The boy bought a .... at the festival.
9 The open air concert is in the .... tomorrow.
10 The talent show finished at .... o'clock.

| 5 |

GOLD experience 2ND EDITION A2 Key for Schools

Name: _____
Class: _____

UNIT 5: SKILLS TEST B

READING

Read the text and answer the questions.

We asked three teenage reporters in London to tell us about an interesting cinema they have been to.

Sam

Yesterday, sixty of us from school went to the cinema. We saw *King Lear*, a film of the Shakespeare play which we're studying this year. The film was a bit too long for me, but I enjoyed it after the film when there was an hour of questions and answers with one of the make-up artists. The cinema where we were is not an ordinary business. All the money it makes goes to a social project in Cambodia.

Rose

On my cousin's birthday last week, her mum took us to an amazing cinema. We were in the open air on the top of a big building. There were fantastic views over London. We weren't sitting in ordinary seats. Everyone had a deck chair, the kind of chair you usually see on a beach or on a ship! They were surprisingly comfortable! There was a huge screen in front of us. We watched a musical comedy. It had great songs and I loved it.

Alex

A couple of months ago, I went with a friend to something called the Secret Cinema. You make a booking and then they email you to say where you will watch the film. We saw a *James Bond* film, in a large old building where they usually keep planes. Everyone in the audience had to dress like a character from the movie and some of the actors were there too. After the film, there was a party and I spoke to one of the main actors. She was really friendly!

Task 1

Choose the correct answer (A, B or C).

Which person:

		Sam	Rose	Alex
11	saw a film with a big group of people?	A	B	C
12	could enjoy looking at the city when they were at the film?	A	B	C
13	had fun at a social event after watching the film?	A	B	C
14	sat on something unusual to watch the film?	A	B	C
15	wanted the film to be shorter?	A	B	C
16	did not know where the film was when they bought tickets?	A	B	C
17	enjoyed watching a funny film?	A	B	C

[ ] 14

Task 2

Answer the questions.

18 Why does Sam say the cinema he went to is not an ordinary business?

....

19 Do you think it was raining when Rose was at the cinema? Why (not)?

....

20 Do you think Alex wore his normal clothes to see the film? Why (not)?

....

[ ] 6

Total: [ ] 50

GOLD experience 2ND EDITION — A2 Key for Schools

Name: _____

Class: _____

UNIT 6: LANGUAGE TEST A

VOCABULARY

Task 1
Choose the correct word to complete the sentences.

1 You go to a railway station to catch a **helicopter / train / bus**.
2 Your **tram / ship / plane** leaves at 8 p.m., so you need to get to the airport at six.
3 It's quicker to go on a **bus / ferry / motorbike** across the lake than to drive all round it.
4 The quickest way to travel across a big city like London is by **bus / underground / ferry**.
5 You must wear a helmet when you ride a **motorbike / coach / helicopter**.
6 I learnt to ride a **car / bike / tram** when I was six years old.
7 I'd love to travel across the Atlantic by **ship / train / coach**.
8 My sister is learning how to fly a **motorbike / helicopter / tram**.
9 A **ferry / coach / tram** is a kind of electric bus that runs along special tracks in some cities.
10 It takes longer to go from the south to the north of the country by **plane / underground / coach**, but it's much cheaper.

[10]

Task 2
Complete the words in the sentences. Use the first letter to help you.

11 We must leave now if we want to **c** _ _ _ _ the last bus.
12 The **f** _ _ _ _ _ from London to Paris only takes about an hour.
13 It's more interesting to go round the city on **f** _ _ _ than to take a bus.
14 Let's take a **t** _ _ _ to the beach tomorrow.
15 It's a long **j** _ _ _ _ _ _ to the mountains, so don't forget your headphones.
16 You can buy your bus **t** _ _ _ _ _ at a machine next to the bus stop.
17 I'd love to **t** _ _ _ _ _ across America by car, wouldn't you?
18 The ferry can't **s** _ _ _ today – it's too windy.
19 Every **p** _ _ _ _ _ _ _ _ in a car should wear a seat belt.
20 Would you like me to **d** _ _ _ _ you to the airport tomorrow or will you take a taxi?

[10]

Task 3
Complete the sentences with these prepositions.

around   by   for   on   to

21 Fiona goes to school .... bus.
22 The train leaves .... four o'clock.
23 It's too far to go to the town centre .... foot.
24 A lot of people were waiting .... the bus to come.
25 I'm going by plane .... London.

[5]

GOLD experience 2ND EDITION A2 Key for Schools

UNIT 6: LANGUAGE TEST A

GRAMMAR

Task 1
Decide if the sentences are talking about intention (I) or prediction (P).
26 The train will probably be late. ....
27 We're going to spend a week in New York in the summer. ....
28 Where are you going to spend the summer? ....
29 What do you think the weather will be like tomorrow? ....
30 The train tickets won't be cheap. ....
31 The children aren't going to watch the film with their parents. ....

Task 2
Write the sentence as either an intention (I) or a prediction (P).
32 My brother / travel / to India / soon. (I)
....
33 I'm sure / you / love / the food in Japan. (P)
....
34 Our neighbours / not / be at home / this weekend. (I)
....
35 Maria and her mother / probably / not spend / very long here. (P)
....
36 Dad / buy / our train tickets / online? (I)
....
37 your visitors / arrive / on time? (P)
....

Task 3
Complete the sentences with the present continuous form of the verbs in brackets.
38 I .... to London tomorrow. (fly)
39 Raj .... Tony this afternoon. (meet)
40 We .... to the meeting. (not / come)
41 What .... on Sunday? (your brother / do)
42 Where .... lunch tomorrow? (you / have)
43 When .... Melbourne? (Tom / leave)
44 Which film .... at the weekend? (the children / watch)

GOLD experience 2ND EDITION A2

UNIT 6: LANGUAGE TEST B

VOCABULARY

Task 1
Choose the correct word to complete the sentences.
1. A **ferry / plane / bike** has wings and you fly in it.
2. A **ferry / ship / motorbike** has two wheels and an engine.
3. A **tram / coach / ship** is a kind of large bus. It often goes from one city to another.
4. When you travel by **tram / coach / underground**, you go down an escalator or a lot of steps to get to a platform.
5. When there is no bridge, people sometimes travel across a river on a **bus / train / ferry**.
6. Riding a **helicopter / bike / coach** is very good exercise.
7. People can sail across the ocean on a **plane / motorbike / ship**.
8. A **coach / ferry / tram** a kind of bus, but it runs on metal tracks.
9. You can fly in a **ship / helicopter / plane**, but it doesn't have any wings.
10. A lot of people are standing on the platform waiting for the **plane / train / bike**.

[10]

Task 2
Complete the words in the sentences. Use the first letter to help you.
11. I got to the airport late and I missed my **f** _ _ _ _ _ to New York.
12. I'd love to be able to **s** _ _ _ a boat, wouldn't you?
13. It's a lovely day. Let's leave the car at home and go to the shops on **f** _ _ _ .
14. It's a long **j** _ _ _ _ _ _ _ from the north of Italy to the south.
15. My class is taking a **t** _ _ _ to the forest tomorrow.
16. My sister learnt to **d** _ _ _ _ a car when she was seventeen.
17. We must leave now or we won't **c** _ _ _ _ the train.
18. There was only one other **p** _ _ _ _ _ _ _ _ on my bus this morning.
19. Do you prefer to **t** _ _ _ _ _ by plane or by train?
20. You must buy your **t** _ _ _ _ _ before you get on the train.

[10]

Task 3
Complete the sentences with these prepositions.

around   by   for   on   to

21. We had a lovely day exploring the city .... foot.
22. We had to wait a long time .... the bus to arrive.
23. The plane leaves .... six o'clock.
24. Are you going by bus .... the airport?
25. I love travelling .... train.

[5]

GOLD experience A2
2ND EDITION — Key for Schools

Name: _____
Class: _____

UNIT 6: LANGUAGE TEST B

GRAMMAR

Task 1
Decide if the sentences are talking about intention (I) or prediction (P).
26 I'm going to visit my grandma this evening. ....
27 What are you going to study at university? ....
28 I think it'll snow tomorrow. ....
29 Who do you think will win the match? ....
30 My parents are not going to buy a new car. ....
31 We won't have time to go shopping at the weekend. ....

[6]

Task 2
Write the sentence as either an intention (I) or a prediction (P).

32 I think / Jack / become / a successful businessman. (P)
....

33 I'm sure / you / enjoy / your trip to New York. (P)
....

34 We / fly / Spain / on Saturday. (I)
....

35 The children / not want / to go / to the city / tomorrow. (P)
....

36 What / you / do / at the weekend? (I)
....

37 I / not spend / my holiday / in France / this year. (I)
....

[12]

Task 3
Complete the sentences with the present continuous form of the verbs in brackets.

38 I .... in the library tomorrow. (study)
39 Meena .... tennis with her cousin on Wednesday. (play)
40 We .... our aunt this weekend. (not / visit)
41 What .... next weekend? (you / do)
42 Where .... her friends this evening? (Hannah / meet)
43 When .... back from Australia? (your grandparents / fly)
44 Which bus .... tomorrow? (your mother / catch)

[7]

Total: [50]

GOLD experience 2ND EDITION A2 Key for Schools

Name: _____

Class: _____

UNIT 6: SKILLS TEST A

DICTATION

You will hear a recording about travel. Listen and write what you hear. You will hear the recording twice.

....

....

....

| 10 |

LISTENING

Listen to Becky telling her father about her friends' holidays.
You will hear the recording twice.

Task 1

Match the people (1–6) with the type of transport (A–H). There are two types of transport you do not need to use.

Person		Type of transport
Example: Abdul	......D......	A plane
1 Bella	....	B train
2 Carlo	....	C ship
3 Diana	....	D helicopter
4 Eddie	....	E bicycle
5 Flora	....	F underground
		G tram
		H coach

| 15 |

Task 2

Complete the sentences.

6 Abdul is going to an ....
7 Bella will visit her ....
8 Diana will travel .... kilometres.
9 Eddie usually travels on the ....
10 Flora will visit her ....

| 5 |

Photocopiable © Pearson Education Limited 2018

GOLD experience 2ND EDITION — A2 Key for Schools

UNIT 6: SKILLS TEST A

READING

Read the interview and answer the questions.

Travel and me

This month we asked Harry, a teenager from London, some questions about travelling.

Do you enjoy travelling?

I enjoy travelling when I'm going on holiday, especially if I'm going somewhere where I can understand a bit of the language. When I'm travelling in a new country, I love looking out of the window of a train or car and seeing how different everything is. But I don't like travelling to school. It's crowded on the bus and the traffic is very slow in the morning.

What's your favourite type of transport?

It's fun going on a plane, but I'm not a fan of waiting for ages at the airport. I like going by boat, too. But once, my uncle took me on the back of his motorbike. That was scary, but brilliant. It's the best way to travel, I think.

Where are you going this year?

In August, my family's going to Edinburgh. It's a beautiful historic city in Scotland. There's a big festival on, and we go every year. This year, my best friend's family is coming with us. There are lots of concerts and plays and comedy shows to go to.

What do you usually take with you when you go travelling?

I always have a bottle of water with me. I also take my phone. I call my friends, of course, but I also use it to write a blog about my travels. I play games on it and I often use a maps app. I leave my laptop at home, but I take my camera. It takes better photos than my phone.

Task 1

Choose the correct answer (A, B or C).

11 What does Harry say he enjoys about travelling?
 A seeing new things
 B watching people
 C learning a new language

12 What kind of transport does Harry like best?
 A boat
 B plane
 C motorbike

13 Why is Harry's family going to Edinburgh?
 A to visit friends
 B to go to some special events
 C to get to know a new city

14 What doesn't Harry take with him when he goes travelling?
 A something to drink
 B a camera
 C a computer

Task 2

Answer the questions.

15 What is it like on Harry's bus to school?
....

16 What does Harry say about travelling by plane?
....

17 What will be different about Harry's holiday in Edinburgh this year?
....

18 Name two things that Harry says he does with his phone (apart from making phone calls).
....

8

Total: 50

12

UNIT 6: SKILLS TEST B

DICTATION

You will hear a recording about travel. Listen and write what you hear. You will hear the recording twice.

....

....

....

[10]

LISTENING

Listen to Becky telling her father about her friends' holidays.
You will hear the recording twice.

Task 1

Match the people (1–6) with the type of transport (A–H). There are two types of transport you do not need to use.

Person

Example: Abdul ....G..........

1 Bella ....
2 Carlo ....
3 Diana ....
4 Eddie ....
5 Flora ....

Type of transport

A bike
B underground
C coach
D tram
E plane
F train
G helicopter
H boat

[15]

Task 2

Complete the sentences.

6 Abdul is feeling ....
7 Bella won't travel by .... this time.
8 Carlo will visit the city of ....
9 Diana is going to the ....
10 Flora's grandmother will take her to visit some ....

[5]

GOLD experience 2ND EDITION A2 Key for Schools

UNIT 6: SKILLS TEST B

READING

Read the interview and answer the questions.

Travel and me

This month we asked Marianne, a teenager from London, some questions about travelling.

Do you enjoy travelling?

I love it. I want to do geography at university. Then I hope I can get a job where I can travel. Perhaps I'll be a tour guide or a travel journalist.

What's your favourite type of transport?

I enjoy flying and going by train and ship. Last year I went in a helicopter for the first time and that was best of all. We had amazing views. We flew over our house and I could see Grandpa sitting in the garden. I'm not a big fan of the underground. It's often so hot and crowded.

Where are you going this year?

In June, Mum and I are going to visit my aunt in St Petersburg in Russia. She teaches English at the university there. We're only going to be there for three days, but I'm looking forward to it very much. That time of year there is called the White Nights because it doesn't get dark at all – the city is so far north.

What do you usually take with you when you go travelling?

I always take my phone. Then I can take photos and listen to music as well as text or phone my friends. I take my headphones and a charger too, of course. I love having things to eat and drink when I travel, but Mum takes all that. Oh, and I always take my diary. I like to write about all the places I go to.

Task 1

Choose the correct answer (A, B or C).

11 What does Marianne want to study when she leaves school?
  A journalism
  B geography
  C tourism

12 What kind of transport does Marianne not like?
  A the underground
  B ship
  C helicopter

13 Why are Marianne and her mother going to Russia?
  A to visit a relative
  B to sightsee in St Petersburg
  C to teach English

14 What doesn't Marianne put in her bag when she goes travelling?
  A a diary
  B headphones
  C a snack

Task 2

Answer the questions.

15 What does Marianne hope to do in her future job?

....

16 What does Marianne say she saw when she was on a helicopter?

....

17 What is special about the 'White Nights' in St Petersburg?

....

18 Name two things that Marianne says she does with her phone (apart from making phone calls).

....

8

Total: 50

12

GOLD experience 2ND EDITION — A2 Key for Schools

Name: _____

Class: _____

UNIT 7: LANGUAGE TEST A

VOCABULARY

Task 1
Match these words with the sentences (1–10).

---
badminton   coach   cycling   diving   helmet
hockey   judo   referee   skiing   surfing
---

1 You need a bike for this sport.
  ....

2 In this sport, you try to hit a ball into a net.
  ....

3 You need a board to do this sport.
  ....

4 Top players of this sport wear a black belt.
  ....

5 You use a racket when you play this sport.
  ....

6 People need to go underwater to do this sport.
  ....

7 You do this sport on snow.
  ....

8 This person helps people get better at a sport.
  ....

9 This person makes decisions about a game (for example, if a goal is really a goal or not).
  ....

10 People wear this on their heads when they do some sports.
  ....

[10]

Task 2
Complete the sentences with the correct form of *do*, *play* or *go*.

11 I .... running every Saturday morning.
12 My brother loves .... judo.
13 Do students at your school .... basketball?
14 My sister .... gymnastics at club near our flat.
15 Do you often .... cycling?
16 Can you .... badminton?
17 Shall we .... skiing together next weekend?
18 I .... diving every day when I was on holiday.

[8]

Task 3
Choose the correct answer (A, B or C).

19 You need a lot of special .... when you go diving.
  A equipment   B rackets   C boards
20 I'm doing an hour of .... at the gym this evening.
  A practise   B practical   C practice
21 It's a good idea to wear a .... when you go cycling.
  A swimsuit   B helmet   C net
22 We use .... to protect our eyes.
  A goggles   B boards   C swimsuits
23 Tennis is played with a .... , but badminton is not.
  A net   B board   C ball
24 I've got football .... tonight.
  A practise   B practical   C practice
25 You play .... with other people.
  A gymnastics   B basketball   C running

[7]

Photocopiable © Pearson Education Limited 2018

GOLD experience
2ND EDITION — A2 Key for Schools

UNIT 7: LANGUAGE TEST A

GRAMMAR

Task 1
Complete the sentences with *can* or *has/have to*.

26 You .... drive on the left in the UK.
27 My little brother .... already play the guitar very well.
28 Most children .... say a few words by the age of 18 months.
29 A referee .... carry a whistle. It's part of the job.
30 Sam .... borrow my pen if he wants.
31 All the students in this school .... wear a uniform. They don't have a choice.

☐ 6

Task 2
Complete the sentences with these words.

_____
             can   can't   could   couldn't
_____

32 We .... play tennis today because it was too wet.
33 Good morning. How .... I help you?
34 I .... go to the party tonight.
35 .... the children go skiing when they were on holiday?
36 Ivan .... speak any English when he arrived in London.
37 I'm sorry, but you .... borrow my bike today. I need to use it.
38 I .... run quickly when I was younger, but I can't now.
39 Climbing a mountain .... sometimes be dangerous.
40 .... you do lots of different sports when you were at school?

☐ 9

Task 3
Complete the email with the correct form of *have to*.

Hi Sam,

My sister and I are really enjoying our new school. You can do lots of different sports here. We all **(41)** .... choose two different sports. I'm doing judo and basketball. I'm on the team for both sports so I go to the sports hall almost every day after **(42)** .... school.

My sister **(43)** .... go there so often. She only **(44)** .... go there twice a week – on Wednesday afternoons and Saturday mornings. She's doing tennis and gymnastics. In our old school, there was no choice: all the boys **(45)** .... play football and all the girls **(46)** .... play hockey.

At my school now, football is very popular, but you **(47)** .... play it if you don't want to. My sister is very happy because she **(48)** .... play hockey here – she hated it at our old school. At least she wasn't in the hockey team, so she **(49)** .... go to matches at the weekends. She's in the tennis team at this school, so she **(50)** .... spend a lot of time practising and playing matches. How are things with you?

All the best,

Tom

☐ 10

Total: ☐ 50

GOLD experience
2ND EDITION — A2 Key for Schools

UNIT 7: LANGUAGE TEST B

VOCABULARY

Task 1
Match these words with the sentences (1–10).

coach   cycling   diving   equipment   helmet
hockey   referee   running   skiing   tennis

1 This sport doesn't need any equipment, and you can do it alone.
....
2 In this sport people hit a ball over a net.
....
3 You go under water when you do this sport.
....
4 This is a word for the things you need – rackets and balls (for example, when you do a sport).
....
5 You sit on something when you do this sport.
....
6 You need to wear this when you do some sports.
....
7 This person teaches people how to play a sport better.
....
8 People usually do this sport in mountains in winter.
....
9 You can play this sport on grass and on ice.
....
10 This person can stop a game if players do something wrong.
....

[10]

Task 2
Complete the sentences with the correct form of *do*, *play* or *go*.

11 My little sister loves .... gymnastics.
12 I .... skiing every weekend in winter.
13 Can you .... judo at the sports club?
14 Do students at your school .... hockey?
15 Do you .... running every day?
16 Can your dad .... basketball well?
17 I .... surfing almost every day last summer
18 Shall we .... cycling together surfing together next weekend?

[8]

Task 3
Choose the correct answer (A, B or C).

19 I've got a black belt in ....
 A gymnastics   B basketball   C judo
20 You need a lot of special .... when you go skiing.
 A equipment   B rackets   C boards
21 I've got hockey .... tonight.
 A practice   B practical   C practise
22 It's important to wear a .... when you go cycling.
 A swimsuit   B helmet   C net
23 I use .... when I go swimming.
 A goggles   B rackets   C nets
24 I hit the ball, but it went into the ....
 A net   B board   C helmet
25 I'm going to basketball .... tonight.
 A practise   B practical   C practice

[7]

GOLD experience 2ND EDITION A2 Key for Schools

UNIT 7: LANGUAGE TEST B

GRAMMAR

Task 1
Complete the sentences with *can* or *has/have to*.

26 Many children .... walk a few steps on their first birthday.
27 A referee .... wear a uniform. It's part of the job.
28 My dad .... drive us home after football today.
29 All the students in this school .... be in their classrooms by 8.45. They have no choice.
30 Your brother .... borrow my tennis racket. I don't need it today.
31 You .... drive on the right in most countries.

Task 2
Complete the sentences with these words.

can   can't   could   couldn't

32 .... I borrow your swimming goggles today?
33 The boys .... go diving today because the weather was so bad.
34 Natasha .... already speak good English when she arrived in the US.
35 I .... understand the rules of cricket. They're too difficult for me.
36 The new sports centre is great. Members .... do lots of different sports there.
37 That man looks like John, but it .... be him. John's in France this week.
38 .... you ride a bike before you started school?
39 We .... swim in the sea yesterday – the water was too cold.
40 .... the children go skiing when they were on holiday?

Task 3
Complete the email with the correct form of *have to*.

Hi Sandra,

I'm going to a special sports school now. It's great. It's very near my house, so I **(41)** .... get a bus to go there. I can walk! I **(42)** .... spend half an hour on the bus every morning to get to my last school.

This week, I **(43)** .... do a project on sports in schools in different countries. How often do you **(44)** .... do sport at your school in New York? Every day? I **(45)** .... do sport every day at my last school, but I do now.

On the first day of term, we all **(46)** .... choose our main sport. I chose gymnastics. My best friend chose badminton. I **(47)** .... go to the gym every week now, but my friend is happy because she **(48)** .... do that.

I **(49)** .... go now. I **(50)** .... do any practice today, but I've got lots of homework!

All the best,

Emily

GOLD experience 2ND EDITION — A2 Key for Schools

Name: _____

Class: _____

UNIT 7: SKILLS TEST A

DICTATION

You will hear a recording about sports. Listen and write what you hear. You will hear the recording twice.

....
....
....

| 10 |

LISTENING

Listen to the five conversations and answer the questions. You will hear the recording twice.

Task 1

Choose the correct picture (A, B or C).

1 What number has Paul got on his basketball shirt?

2 What is Sandro's favourite sport?

3 What did Melissa buy at the sports shop?

4 What time does the hockey game start?

5 Which sport can Zara do well?

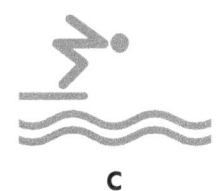

| 15 |

Task 2

Answer the questions.

6 What number has Tom got on his basketball shirt? ....
7 What is Leila's favourite sport? ....
8 What did Melissa want at the sports shop? ....
9 When does Ned need to be at the hockey practice? ....
10 What sport will Zara and Charlie do at the weekend? ....

| 5 |

Photocopiable © Pearson Education Limited 2018

GOLD experience
2ND EDITION — A2 Key for Schools

Name: _____
Class: _____

UNIT 7: SKILLS TEST A

READING

Read the text and answer the questions.

Task 1

Choose the correct answer (A, B or C) for each gap.

Sports Camp, Scotland

In the mountains of Scotland, there is a very popular sports camp. Students go there in their school holidays to **(11)** .... There are all sorts of different sports, such as mountain **(12)** ...., mountain biking and skiing. The camp has lots of very good **(13)** .... for everyone to use. Students also learn other **(14)** .... that are very important for people who are keen on sport (refereeing and **(15)** ...., for example). If they **(16)** .... one of these courses, they can then get work in sports clubs. Lots of students like to do this because they can then earn a bit of money in their **(17)** .... time when they go back home. Students at this sports camp are **(18)** .... all the time, but they love it.

11	A make	B get	C do
12	A going	B climbing	C travelling
13	A staff	B furniture	C equipment
14	A skills	B studies	C exercises
15	A coaching	B lesson	C club
16	A end	B complete	C miss
17	A empty	B other	C free
18	A full	B busy	C fast

[16]

Task 2

Answer the questions.

19 What can students learn at this sports camp?

....

20 What can happen to students who learn these different things?

....

[4]

Total: [50]

72 Photocopiable © Pearson Education Limited 2018

GOLD experience 2ND EDITION — A2 Key for Schools

Name: _____
Class: _____

UNIT 7: SKILLS TEST B

DICTATION

You will hear a recording about sports. Listen and write what you hear. You will hear the recording twice.

....
....
....

[10]

LISTENING

Listen to the five conversations and answer the questions. You will hear the recording twice.

Task 1

Choose the correct picture (A, B or C).

1 What number has Tom got on his basketball shirt? 
   A (10)   B (15)   C (18)

2 What is Leila's favourite sport?
   A (tennis)   B (cycling)   C (basketball)

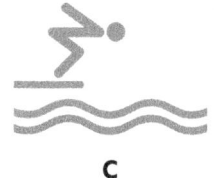

3 What does the boy want to buy at the sports shop? 
   A (goggles)   B (surfboard)   C (swimsuit)

4 What time must Ned be at the hockey field?
   A 6.00   B 7.30   C 8.00

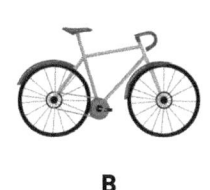

5 Which sport can Charlie do well? 
   A (diving)   B (running)   C (swimming)

[15]

Task 2

Answer the questions.

6 What number has Paul got on his basketball shirt?   ....
7 What is Sandro's favourite sport?   ....
8 What did Melissa buy at the sports shop?   ....
9 When does Ned's hockey practice start?   ....
10 What sport will Zara watch in the afternoon?   ....

[5]

GOLD experience 2ND EDITION — A2 Key for Schools

UNIT 7: SKILLS TEST B

READING

Read the text and answer the questions.

Task 1

Choose the correct answer (A, B or C) for each gap.

Sports Camp, Scotland

In the north of Scotland there is a very popular sports camp. It specialises in water sports – diving, **(11)** .... and water-skiing. Students love going there in their school holidays. It isn't expensive and they can **(12)** .... , lots of different sports. The camp has excellent **(13)** .... to help them improve their **(14)** .... It also has the latest **(15)** .... for everyone to use. Students at this sports camp are **(16)** .... all the time. In the evenings, they can learn things like refereeing or sports journalism that will help them if they want a career in sport. If they **(17)** .... one of these courses, they can then earn a bit of money in their **(18)** .... time when they go back home.

11	A riding	B sailing	C basketball
12	A do	B make	C get
13	A trains	B coaches	C workers
14	A exercises	B studies	C skills
15	A furniture	B equipment	C staff
16	A fast	B full	C busy
17	A miss	B complete	C end
18	A free	B empty	C other

[16]

Task 2

Answer the questions.

19 What can students learn at this sports camp?

....

20 What can happen to students who learn these different things?

....

[4]

Total: [50]

GOLD experience 2ND EDITION — A2 Key for Schools

Name: _____
Class: _____

UNIT 8: LANGUAGE TEST A

VOCABULARY

Task 1
Complete the sentences with one word.
1. A sea between continents is an ………………… .
2. A long area of water from the moutains to the sea is a ………………… .
3. A very hot and dry place with no trees is a ………………… .
4. An area of land with water around it is an ………………… .
5. An area of water with land around it is a ………………… .

[5]

Task 2
Look at the pictures and complete the weather words.

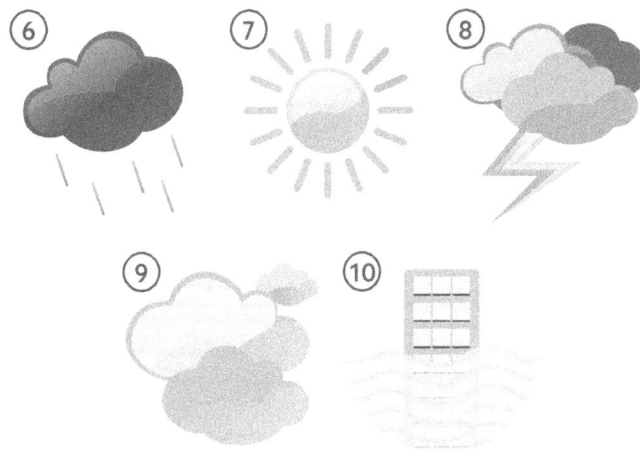

6. _ a _ _
7. _ u _
8. _ _ _ r _
9. c _ _ _ _
10. _ _ g
11. _ _ o _
12. _ i _ _
13. _ c _

[8]

Task 3
Choose the correct word to complete the sentences.
14. This food is boiling **hot** / **cold**. I can't eat it.
15. It's freezing **cool** / **cold** outside. Put on a coat!
16. It's quite **cold** / **warm** outside so I'll wear a T-shirt.
17. I would like a nice **warm** / **cool** drink, like lemonade.
18. I'm feeling **hot** / **cold**. Can you open the window, please?

[5]

Task 4
Complete the sentences with these words.

cloudy   dry   fog   ice   rains   wet   wind

19. It ………………… a lot in November.
20. There was a lot of ………………… this morning, and it was difficult to see anything.
21. It's dangerous to drive when there is ………………… on the road.
22. The seat was …………………, so I didn't sit on it.
23. It was ………………… today, and the sky looked very dark.
24. I hope it's ………………… tomorrow, because I want to go for a walk in the mountains.
25. There was a strong ………………… today, and it felt cold.

[7]

GOLD experience 2ND EDITION A2

UNIT 8: LANGUAGE TEST A

GRAMMAR

Task 1
Complete the sentences with *have* or *has*.

26 You .... visited a lot of interesting places.
27 Both my brothers .... gone to university.
28 .... your mother ever been to Japan?
29 I .... never seen an iceberg.
30 Suzanna .... swum with dolphins.
31 What .... the children done today?

[6]

Task 2
Write the past participles of these verbs.

32 ride ....
33 learn ....
34 put ....
35 make ....
36 have ....

37 buy ....
38 write ....
39 read ....
40 eat ....
41 stop ....

[10]

Task 3
Complete the blog with the present perfect form of the words in brackets.

Yesterday, I had a very interesting talk with my grandfather. He **(42)** .... (have) a very interesting life. He **(43)** .... (be) to all of the continents except Antarctica.

He and my grandma **(44)** .... (visit) some amazing places. Grandma says that Iceland is the most interesting country she **(45)** .... (ever / see). They often go back there because they **(46)** .... (make) some very good friends there. Their friends **(47)** .... (often / come) to this country, too, and **(48)** .... (tell) me a lot about their country.

My grandpa **(49)** .... (write) a book about their travels. I **(50)** .... (not read) it yet, but I am going to take it on holiday and read it then.

[9]

Total: [50]

GOLD experience 2ND EDITION — A2 Key for Schools

Name: _____
Class: _____

UNIT 8: LANGUAGE TEST B

VOCABULARY

Task 1
Complete the sentences with one word.
1 An area of high land, like a mountain, is a ....
2 A hot, wet place with lots of trees is a ....
3 The place where land meets the sea is the ....
4 A hot, dry place with no trees is a ....
5 A large sea is an ....

[ ] 5

Task 2
Look at the pictures and complete the weather words.

6 r _ _ _
7 _ _ n
8 _ t _ _ _
9 _ l _ _ _
10 f _ _
11 _ n _ _
12 _ _ _ d
13 i _ _

[ ] 8

Task 3
Choose the correct word to complete the sentences.
14 This food is **boiling** / **freezing** hot. I can't eat it.
15 I'm feeling **hot** / **cold**. Can you close the window, please?
16 This soup isn't **warm** / **cool**. It's cold.
17 It's not raining, it's **wet** / **dry**.
18 It's **boiling** / **freezing** cold outside. Put on a coat!

[ ] 5

Task 4
Complete the sentences with these words.

fog   ice   snows   snowy   sun   sunny

19 It .... a lot in the winter.
20 There was a lot of .... today, and it was difficult to see.
21 The .... only came out for ten minutes today!
22 It was very .... last night, and now everything looks white.
23 It was .... today, and the sky looked very dark.
24 It was .... this morning, so I went running in the park.
25 Don't drive when there is .... on the road.

[ ] 7

Photocopiable © Pearson Education Limited 2018

GOLD experience 2ND EDITION A2

UNIT 8: LANGUAGE TEST B

GRAMMAR

Task 1
Complete the sentences with *have* or *has*.

26 I .... never been to Australia.
27 My parents .... climbed Mount Kilimanjaro.
28 Henry .... gone home.
29 Where .... you been?
30 We .... had a very interesting day today.
31 .... your brother seen a lot of wild animals?

6

Task 2
Write the past participles of these verbs.

32 fly ....
33 buy ....
34 swim ....
35 take ....
36 write ....

37 wear ....
38 eat ....
39 see ....
40 hear ....
41 do ....

10

Task 3
Complete the blog with the present perfect form of the words in brackets.

I **(42)** .... (always / want) to go to Japan. My brother **(43)** .... (go) to Tokyo and he **(44)** .... (tell) me a lot about it. I **(45)** .... (see) some fantastic TV programmes about the country and I **(46)** .... (also / read) a very good book about Japanese history. I **(47)** .... (start) going to Japanese lessons, but I **(48)** .... (learn) much yet. It's a very difficult language, I think. We **(49)** .... (have) French lessons at school for three years now and that is much easier. No one in my family **(50)** .... (ever / visit) France, but we hope to go there next year.

9

Total: 50

GOLD experience 2ND EDITION A2 Key for Schools

Name:
Class:

UNIT 8: SKILLS TEST A

DICTATION

You will hear a recording about a holiday. Listen and write what you hear. You will hear the recording twice.

....

....

....

[10]

LISTENING

You will hear Kirsty and Tom talking about their family's trip to South Africa.
You will hear the recording twice.

Task 1

Choose the correct answer (A, B or C).

1 What did Tom enjoy doing on the flight?
   A looking at the view
   B eating interesting food
   C watching movies

2 What was the weather like when they arrived?
   A dry
   B cool
   C windy

3 Which animals did Kirsty like most?
   A lions
   B elephants
   C monkeys

4 What did they do on Sunday?
   A They walked in a desert.
   B They climbed a mountain.
   C They swam in a lake.

5 Which sport did Kirsty and Tom's father not do?
   A canoeing
   B diving
   C surfing

[15]

Task 2

Answer the questions.

6 What did Kirsty like doing on the flight?
7 How was the weather when they arrived?
8 What animals did Tom like most?
9 What did they do on Friday?
10 What sport did Kirsty and Tom's mother not do?

....
....
....
....
....

[5]

GOLD experience
2ND EDITION — A2 Key for Schools

UNIT 8: SKILLS TEST A

READING

Read the text and answer the questions.

World Rivers Day

Did you know that the fourth Sunday in September is World Rivers Day? It's a day to celebrate rivers and all they do for us. We asked three teenagers to tell us about a river that they know.

Tanya

My aunt lives in the city of Shanghai near the longest river in Asia. It's called the Chang Jiang, which means 'long river' in Chinese. Last summer my aunt and I went on a ship on the river. We sailed through some very unusual and very beautiful mountains in one part of our trip. It was cloudy every day, but I still got some amazing photos.

Sam

Last year I read a very funny story about three men and a dog. They sailed up the River Thames in England. I haven't sailed on the Thames, but I have gone fishing there. I didn't catch anything, but I enjoyed sitting by the river in the sunshine looking at lots of interesting birds. I've also walked along the Thames in London.

Grace

I often go to a little town in the south of France. It's by the sea not far from some mountains. In winter a river runs through the town, but in summer the river bed is usually completely dry and cars can park on it! One day last summer it rained very heavily and the river filled up with water again. I saw cars moving down the river like little boats.

Task 1

Choose the correct answer (A, B or C).

Which person:

	Tanya	Sam	Grace
11 has done some sport on a river?	A	B	C
12 has seen something unusual in a river?	A	B	C
13 got some good pictures of a river?	A	B	C
14 talks about a sunny day by a river?	A	B	C
15 has been on a boat on a river?	A	B	C
16 says a river is very different at different times of the year?	A	B	C
17 enjoyed a book about a river?	A	B	C

[14]

Task 2

Answer the questions.

18 When is World Rivers Day?

....

19 What is the English translation of the name of Tanya's river?

....

20 Where is the town that Grace visits in the south of France?

....

[6]

Total: [50]

UNIT 8: SKILLS TEST B

DICTATION

You will hear a recording about a holiday. Listen and write what you hear. You will hear the recording twice.

....

....

....

| 10 |

LISTENING

You will hear Kirsty and Tom talking about their family's trip to South Africa.
You will hear the recording twice.

Task 1

For each question choose the correct answer (A, B or C).

1 What did Kirsty enjoy doing on the flight?
   A looking at the view
   B eating interesting food
   C watching movies

2 What was the weather like when they arrived?
   A wet
   B hot
   C windy

3 Which animals did Tom like most?
   A lions
   B elephants
   C monkeys

4 What did they do on Saturday?
   A They walked in a desert.
   B They climbed a mountain.
   C They swam in a lake.

5 Which sport did Kirsty and Tom's mother not do?
   A canoeing
   B surfing
   C diving

| 15 |

Task 2

Answer the questions.

6 What did Tom like doing on the flight?
7 How did they expect the weather to be when they arrived?
8 What animals did Kirsty like most?
9 What did they do on Sunday?
10 What sport did Kirsty and Tom's father not do?

| 5 |

GOLD experience 2ND EDITION — A2 Key for Schools

UNIT 8: SKILLS TEST B

READING

Read the text and answer the questions.

International Mountain Day

Did you know that 11 December is International Mountains Day? It's a day to celebrate mountains and the people who live in mountainous areas. We asked three teenagers to tell us about a mountain that they know.

Tricia

Last year I watched a very interesting movie about a man who climbed mountains. He has climbed the highest mountains in the world, but when he was younger, he trained by climbing a mountain only a few kilometres from where I live! There is a train which goes all the way to the top! It's great at the top, and there's even a little café there. I got some postcards! Of course, there are difficult paths going up the mountain, but on the other side.

Rachel

My brother lives in the Japanese city of Tokyo, near one of the most famous mountains in the world. It's Mount Fuji, and you can see it from Tokyo. Last summer I went there with him. It's only possible to climb up the mountain in the summer because there is snow at other times of the year. It was sunny at the top and I got some amazing photos.

Greg

I often go to a little town in the south of France. It's not far from some mountains. There's a mountain there called Mont Ventoux, and it's very high. You can see it from all over the countryside. It's famous for people who want to train to do the *Tour de France* – the famous bike race. Once, I was driving up the mountain with my father, and we were stuck behind about ten or twenty cyclists. It was amazing that they could cycle so high up a mountain.

Task 1

Choose the correct answer (A, B or C).

Which person:	Tricia	Rachel	Greg
11 has gone up a mountain without using transport?	A	B	C
12 has seen something unusual on a mountain?	A	B	C
13 has seen a mountain from a city?	A	B	C
14 has bought something on a mountain?	A	B	C
15 has been in a car on a mountain?	A	B	C
16 says a mountain is different at different times of the year?	A	B	C
17 enjoyed a film about a mountain?	A	B	C

[ ] 14

Task 2

Answer the questions.

18 When is International Mountain Day?

....

19 Why is Mont Ventoux used by cyclists?

....

20 What did Rachel do at the top of Mount Fuji?

....

[ ] 6

Total: [ ] 50

GOLD experience 2ND EDITION — A2 Key for Schools

Name: _____
Class: _____

UNIT 9: LANGUAGE TEST A

VOCABULARY

Task 1
Answer the questions with these words.

cake   cereal   chips   omelette   pasta   salad   sandwich   soup   steak

Which food ...
1 is made from potatoes? ....
2 is mostly made from eggs? ....
3 is two pieces of bread with something in the middle? ....
4 do people drink or eat with a spoon? ....
5 do people often have on their birthday? ....
6 is sometimes lettuce, tomato and cucumber? ....
7 can be, for example, spaghetti or macaroni? ....
8 is a large piece of meat? ....
9 do people sometimes have with milk at breakfast? ....

[9]

Task 2
Choose the correct words to complete the text.

Let's **(10) have / go** breakfast now – coffee, toast and some **(11) fried / fresh** fruit – and then **(12) go / go** for a walk. I think I need some fresh **(13) time / air**. And we both need to **(14) make / get** some exercise. But I also need to **(15) find / do** time to relax, too!

[6]

Task 3
Put the capital letters in the correct order to make a word to complete the sentences.

16 If you have .... you should go to the dentist.   A E T T C O H H O
17 My dad .... very good cakes.   S B E A K
18 The boy has eaten so much ice cream that he is now feeling ....   I K S C
19 Try not to have .... between meals.   S S A K C N
20 Fried food isn't very ....   Y A L E H Y H
21 It's nice to cook a .... in the garden.   E B U A R C B E
22 You feel very warm – have you got a .... ?   R U M P T E E R E A U
23 Green .... are very good for you.   S E T B V L A G E E
24 You need to .... the egg for around three minutes.   L I O B
25 Would you like a .... with your cup of tea?   I T S U B C I

[10]

GOLD experience 2ND EDITION — A2 Key for Schools

UNIT 9: LANGUAGE TEST A

GRAMMAR

Task 1
Complete the first conditional sentences with the correct form of the word in brackets.

26 Clare .... more swimming competitions if she practises more. (win)
27 They'll buy something to eat if they .... hungry. (get)
28 I .... to school tomorrow if my cold gets worse. (not go)
29 If my parents .... me a new phone for my birthday, I'll be very surprised. (give)
30 If I invite you to my party, ... ? (you / come)
31 We won't play tennis tonight if you .... tired. (be)
32 If Sally goes to bed early tonight, she .... better tomorrow. (feel)
33 The children will be late for school if they .... immediately. (not leave)
34 I .... an omelette if we go to the French restaurant this evening. (have)
35 Mum will be very happy if Tom .... dinner tomorrow. (cook)

[10]

Task 2
Make first conditional sentences.

36 if / Lisa / have a cold / I / look after the children / .
....
37 you / need / your umbrella / if you / go out / today / .
....
38 what / the teacher / say / if / the children / not do / their homework / ?
....
39 if / I / make a cheese sandwich / you / have one / too / ?
....
40 the new restaurant / open / next Monday / if / everything / be / ready / .
....

[10]

Task 3
Complete these pieces of advice with *should* or *shouldn't*.

41 It's your aunt's birthday next week – we .... send her a card.
42 You .... drink a lot of sweet drinks.
43 Paul has a bad cold – he .... have a honey and lemon drink.
44 I .... spend so much money on clothes. I haven't got any money left!
45 We .... try the new cafe in town – it looks very nice.

[5]

Total: [50]

GOLD experience 2ND EDITION — A2 Key for Schools

Name: _____
Class: _____

UNIT 9: LANGUAGE TEST B

VOCABULARY

Task 1
Answer the questions with these words.

cake   cereal   chips   omelette   pasta   salad   sandwich   soup   steak

Which food …
1. comes from a cow? ....
2. contains two or more different vegetables or fruit? ....
3. can be, for example, ravioli or spaghetti? ....
4. is bread with, for example, cheese or meat? ....
5. is, for example, cornflakes or muesli? ....
6. is a kind of fried potato? ....
7. usually has sugar in it? ....
8. can people eat or drink? ....
9. is mostly made from eggs? ....

☐ 9

Task 2
Choose the correct words to complete the text.

We **(10) had / did** breakfast at 7.30. I just had some **(11) fried / fresh** fruit, but my friend had some **(12) fried / green** food. Not so healthy! Then we **(13) went / went** for a walk. We both wanted to **(14) make / get** a bit of exercise. I needed to **(15) get / do** some fresh air, and my friend just wanted to feel better after his big breakfast!

☐ 6

Task 3
Put the capital letters in the correct order to make a word to complete the sentences.

16. It is important for everyone to find .... to relax.   E M I T
17. I love to .... fish.   L G I R L
18. My mum loves to .... her own bread.   E B A K
19. The children usually want a .... – an apple or some chocolate, perhaps – when they come home from school.   S C A N K
20. If you eat too much you will get .... ache.   M O S A T C H
21. I think .... potatoes are healthier than fried.   L O B I D E
22. Jack loves to have a .... for dinner.   R U G B E R
23. In summer it's fun to .... food outside.   R U B A C U B E
24. I feel .... after all that cake.   I K S C
25. I feel hot. I think I've got a ....   E T R E M U P T E A R

☐ 10

GOLD experience 2ND EDITION A2

UNIT 9: LANGUAGE TEST B

GRAMMAR

Task 1
Complete the first conditional sentence with the correct form of the word in brackets.

26 You .... better if you eat more fruit and vegetables. (feel)
27 They'll go to bed early if they .... tired. (be)
28 We .... swimming in the sea tomorrow if it's cold and wet again. (not go)
29 Suzie won't come to the party if she .... a toothache. (have)
30 If I barbecue the burgers, ... a salad? (make, you)
31 We won't go to that restaurant if you .... to. (not want)
32 If Alex has a lot of maths homework today, dad .... him with it. (help)
33 If Anna .... the house now, she'll miss her flight. (not leave)
34 I think I .... pasta if we go to the Italian restaurant. (have)
35 The children will get cold today if they .... warm clothes. (not wear)

10

Task 2
Make first conditional sentences.

36 I / buy / the cinema tickets / if / they / be / not too expensive / .
....

37 if / it / be / a nice day on Saturday / we / go to the beach / .
....

38 what / Mike / say / if / the girls / get home / late / ?
....

39 if / the students / do / well / in their exam / the teacher / show / them a film / .
....

40 if / Mary / go for a walk / this evening / you / go / with her / ?
....

10

Task 3
Complete these pieces of advice with *should* or *shouldn't*.

41 Everyone .... eat lots of vegetables every day. They're good for us!
42 You .... eat snacks between meals. It's not healthy.
43 Maria has a bad stomach ache – she .... go to the doctor.
44 You .... read in the dark. It's bad for your eyes.
45 We .... wash the vegetables before cooking them. It's not nice to eat dirty food.

5

Total: 50

GOLD experience
2ND EDITION — A2 Key for Schools

UNIT 9: SKILLS TEST A

DICTATION

You will hear a recording about eating. Listen and write what you hear. You will hear the recording twice.

....

....

....

[10]

LISTENING

You will hear a teacher telling her class about a cooking lesson.
You will hear the recording twice.

Task 1
Complete the information. Write one word, or a number, or a date, or a time.

Special cooking lesson (Group A)	
Day of lesson:	(1) ....
Time of lesson:	(2) ....
Bring:	(3) some .... and (4) .... grams of sugar
This group will make:	(5) ....

[10]

Task 2
Complete the sentences.

6 Group B's lesson will be on ....
7 The time of Group B's lesson is at a quarter past ....
8 Students in Group B should bring some ....
9 They should also bring .... grams of sugar.
10 Group B is going to make ....

[10]

GOLD experience
2ND EDITION — A2 Key for Schools

UNIT 9: SKILLS TEST A

READING

Read the text and answer the questions.

TV Food Programmes

In the last ten years or so, British people have stopped buying so much bread and so many cakes and biscuits from the supermarket and have started making them at home. This is largely because of the popularity of a TV programme called *The Great British Bake-Off*.

Since it began, lots of different countries have bought the format. You can now watch similar shows in lots of different places including Argentina, France, South Africa and the USA. Each year, the show starts with about twelve competitors. They are all ordinary people who love baking. Each week, they have to do a different task for the judges. At the end of each programme, the judges tell one person to leave the show. At the end of ten programmes, one person wins the title of Best British Baker.

Why do people love this programme? It's interesting watching people make beautiful and delicious things. And it's exciting – who will have to leave next? It makes people want to try some of the recipes themselves, and encouraging people to enjoy baking is in my opinion a good thing, even if supermarkets may not agree.

But people also like it when there is a problem in the studio kitchen. Audiences seem to love it when someone cuts their finger or drops a cake on the floor. It may seem surprising, but sometimes there is a lot of drama in this show!

Task 1
Choose the correct answer (A, B or C).

11 What does the writer say British people do more now?
  A buy bread
  B eat cakes
  C bake biscuits

12 Which of these people can be a competitor on the TV show?
  A a professional cook
  B a police officer
  C a celebrity

13 In the third paragraph, the writer is pleased that
  A cooking is becoming a more popular activity.
  B his own baking skills have improved a lot.
  C some bakers have to leave the programme.

14 What does the writer say may surprise readers?
  A Not many competitors get nervous and drop things.
  B Exciting things can happen in the programme.
  C Viewers like it when people make mistakes.

[12]

Task 2
Answer the questions.

15 When did the TV show start?
....

16 How do we know the show is popular?
....

17 Why is the show exciting?
....

18 What does the writer think is a good thing about the show?
....

[8]

Total: [50]

GOLD experience
2ND EDITION — A2 Key for Schools

Name: _____

Class: _____

UNIT 9: SKILLS TEST B

DICTATION

You will hear a recording about eating. Listen and write what you hear. You will hear the recording twice.

....

....

....

[ ] 10

LISTENING

You will hear a teacher telling her class about a cooking lesson.
You will hear the recording twice.

Task 1

Complete the information. Write one word, or a number, or a date, or a time.

Special cooking lesson (Group B)	
Day of lesson:	(1) ....
Time of lesson:	(2) ....
Bring:	(3) some .... and (4) .... grams of sugar
This group will make:	(5) ....

[ ] 10

Task 2

Complete the sentences.

6 Group A's lesson will be on ....
7 The time of Group A's lesson is at a quarter to ....
8 Students in Group A should bring some ....
9 They should also bring .... grams of sugar.
10 Group A is going to make ....

[ ] 10

Photocopiable © Pearson Education Limited 2018

GOLD experience
2ND EDITION — A2 Key for Schools

UNIT 9: SKILLS TEST B

READING

Read the text and answer the questions.

TV *MasterChef*

People sometimes say that we cook much less at home these days. We often go out to restaurants or buy takeaways, but the strange thing is that we watch far more TV about cooking. *MasterChef* is one of the most popular TV programmes in the world. It is a cooking competition and it was first on TV in Britain in 1990. You can see it now in forty different countries all over the world, including Brazil, India and Russia. It is especially popular in Australia.

In each programme, cooks have to do different tasks and at the end of most of the shows, the judges tell someone to leave. After about twenty programmes, the most successful cook wins the title of MasterChef.

There are four different forms of the show. There is the 'ordinary' *MasterChef*. Then there is *MasterChef Professional* for people who already work in restaurants. There is *Celebrity MasterChef* which is for famous people who also love cooking. There is also *Junior MasterChef* for cooks up to the age of sixteen.

Why is the show so popular? Perhaps it is because people travel more these days. They enjoy eating foreign food and they want to learn how to cook it. Also, we can also buy all sorts of international ingredients in our shops. It is good that people enjoy watching programmes like *MasterChef*. Eating well is good for our health. So if the programme makes people think more carefully about what they eat, that will be a good thing.

Task 1
Choose the correct answer (A, B or C).

11 In the first paragraph, why does the writer think it is strange that *MasterChef* is popular?
  A because it has been on TV for a very long time
  B because people do not cook at home so much now
  C because there are so many cooking programmes on TV

12 Which country had *MasterChef* on TV first?
  A Australia
  B Brazil
  C Britain

13 Which is the right *MasterChef* for a 1990s pop star who would like to buy a restaurant?
  A *Junior MasterChef*
  B *MasterChef Professional*
  C *Celebrity MasterChef*

14 The writer says it is good that people enjoy watching cooking programmes because
  A it may make them healthier.
  B it may make them eat more international food.
  C it may teach them useful skills.

[12]

Task 2
Answer the questions.

15 When did the TV show start?
....

16 How do we know the show is popular?
....

17 Who is *Junior MasterChef* good for?
....

18 What does the writer think is a good thing about the show?
....

[8]

Total: [50]

REVIEW (UNITS 1–3): LANGUAGE TEST A

VOCABULARY

Task 1
Complete the sentences with the correct words. Use the first letter to help you.

1 When I'm in a quiet place I use **h**............................ to listen to music.
2 I taught my gran how to use a **m**............................ to point at the words on her computer screen.
3 Dad put up a **b**............................ on my bedroom wall, so I can put all my dictionaries and school books there.
4 In **g**............................ today we studied famous rivers.
5 We're going **c**............................ at the weekend in a very big tent.
6 My friend loves **b**............................ and brings lovely chocolate cakes into school for us every Monday.
7 I went on a **s**............................ at my friend's house last night and we watched lots of films before bed!

[7]

Task 2
Choose the correct verb to complete the sentences.

8 We **wear / get** red shirts when we play football.
9 I usually **do / get** my homework with my friend at her house.
10 How often do you **play / go** computer games?
11 I never **have / get** bored in science lessons.
12 I don't **collect / chat** comics, but my sister does, and she's got over 200.
13 Can you **chat / message** Peter and tell him that we're late for football practice?
14 My mum and dad **go / collect** shopping for food on Friday evenings.
15 It's good to **go / chat** with friends online when you can't see them very often.

[8]

Task 3
Choose the correct answer (A, B or C).

16 How often do you .... this website?
   A go   **B** visit   **C** stream
17 I've got an amazing new .... for my phone.
   A website   **B** email   **C** app
18 There's a .... from Mum on the table.
   A card   **B** note   **C** email
19 I got .... late yesterday.
   A home   **B** house   **C** bedroom
20 The .... on my tablet is great for reading.
   A mouse   **B** webcam   **C** screen
21 I often get useful information and books from the ....
   A café   **B** bookshelf   **C** library
22 The teacher wants us to make a .... in class this week.
   A video   **B** project   **C** test
23 To be a doctor, you've got to study ....
   A history   **B** art   **C** biology
24 There were two new .... in our class this week. They're both the same age as me.
   A desks   **B** pupils   **C** teachers
25 Do you want to .... to the cinema this weekend?
   A get   **B** make   **C** go

[10]

GOLD experience A2
2ND EDITION — Key for Schools

Name: _____
Class: _____

REVIEW (UNITS 1–3): LANGUAGE TEST A

GRAMMAR

Task 1
Put the words in the correct order to make sentences.

26 go / often / she / shopping / does / How / ?

27 you / friend / did / visit / your / When / ?

28 do / I / the / my / evening / usually / in / homework / .

29 working / now / your / in / dad / Is / London / ?

30 have / on / don't / Maths / Fridays / We / .

Task 2
Complete the sentences with the correct form of the verbs in brackets.

31 .... (you / enjoy) going to the cinema?
32 My sister .... (not / like) painting, but she .... (love) drawing.
33 Frank .... (not / learn) learn English when he .... (be) at primary school five years ago.
34 .... (you / do) your homework at the moment?
35 Where .... (you / go) for your last holiday?
36 I .... (not / watch) TV at the moment because I .... (read) reading a book.

Task 3
For each question write the correct answer. Write one word for each gap.

Hi Luke,

Hey! I've got **(37)** .... new French friends! I **(38)** .... on holiday in Paris last week and I met them at a concert. They were in **(39)** .... of me. Now we chat online every day – in French! My French **(40)** .... getting better, and their English, too.

Message me and tell me all about your holiday. **(41)** .... you have a lot of fun?

Love, Sara

GOLD experience 2ND EDITION A2 Key for Schools

REVIEW (UNITS 1–3): LANGUAGE TEST B

VOCABULARY

Task 1
Complete the sentences with the correct words. Use the first letter to help you.

1 I need a new **k**.......................... for my computer because some of the letters don't work now.
2 We've got our new **t**.......................... at school today and I love Wednesdays because we've got sport and art – my favourite subjects.
3 My friend likes **s**.......................... – she's got a beautiful voice.
4 The **u**.......................... at my new school is a black skirt or trousers with a white shirt.
5 I need a laptop with a bigger **s**.......................... because on this one, the words are hard to read.
6 In **b**.......................... lessons, I prefer studying the human body to studying flowers and trees.
7 My brother loves superhero films, like *Spiderman*, and he's read all the **c**.......................... they were in.

[7]

Task 2
Choose the correct verb to complete the sentences.

8 The school bus is at 3.30 so I never **go / get** home before 4.15.
9 **Chat / Click** on the link in this email and you can watch the video.
10 We always **have / collect** a lot of homework at the weekends, but I never do it before Sunday evening.
11 The pupils in my country don't usually **play / wear** a uniform to school.
12 I often **play / do** cards with my sisters when we're on holiday.
13 Jacky didn't **get / make** a good mark for her History test because she didn't study for it.
14 My mum and dad **collect / play** postcards and they've got one from nearly every country in the world.
15 I sometimes **go / play** on a sleepover at my friend's and we usually have great fun!

[8]

Task 3
Choose the correct answer (A, B or C).

16 Sometimes I don't go out at the weekend and I .... bored.
  A go B do C get
17 I love this .... on my phone because it tells me about new music.
  A tablet B email C app
18 We wrote a lot of English sentences in our .... today.
  A marks B notebooks C rulers
19 This website is good and a lot of people .... it.
  A go B visit C message
20 We don't watch TV now because we .... programmes on our laptop.
  A stream B email C listen
21 In .... today we learned about towns in Australia.
  A geography B physics C maths
22 There's a letter for your parents in the school ....
  A library B gym C office
23 How often do you .... cartoons on TV?
  A watch B listen C read
24 I .... shopping last Saturday and I bought a new phone.
  A went B got C visited
25 I sometimes do my homework in the .... because it's quiet.
  A desk B library C timetable

[10]

GOLD experience 2ND EDITION — A2 Key for Schools

Name: _____
Class: _____

REVIEW (UNITS 1-3): LANGUAGE TEST B

GRAMMAR

Task 1
Put the words in the correct order to make sentences.

26 don't / after / We / shopping / school / go / often / .

....

27 working / laptop / the / isn't / at / moment / My / .

....

28 us / today / teacher / any / Did / the / give / homework / .

....

29 enjoy / Do / online / you / chatting / ?

....

30 doesn't / cheese / brother / sandwiches / like / My / brother / .

....

[10]

Task 2
Complete the sentences with the correct form of the verbs in brackets.

31 We .... (not / have) art this morning, but we .... (have) sport.
32 I .... (usually / go) to school by bus, but today I .... (walk). It was fine.
33 .... (your dad / drive) at the moment?
34 My sister .... (love) going to the cinema with her friends on Saturday.
35 .... (you / send) any postcards when you .... (be) on holiday last week?
36 I .... (not / enjoy) learning French, but I .... (like) learning Italian!

[10]

Task 3
For each question write the correct answer. Write one word for each gap.

Hi Danny,

I hope you had a good holiday **(37)** .... week! **(38)** .... you go to the concert in London?

I went to Spain with my family and I met a nice Spanish girl, Maria. She was next to me on the plane. She didn't speak much English, so I **(39)** .... teaching her. My Spanish is OK, but I'd like to improve. Maria **(40)** .... helping me too. We are good online friends now.

(41) .... you speak Spanish? When she visits me in England next year, you can meet her.

Love, Max

[5]

Total: [50]

REVIEW (UNITS 1–3): WRITING AND SPEAKING

WRITING

You want to tell your cousin Mark, about your weekend with a friend.
Write an email to Mark.
In your email:

- tell Mark who you stayed with and where he/she lives
- say what you did
- ask Mark about his weekend

Write **25 words** or more on a separate answer sheet.

GOLD experience 2ND EDITION — A2 Key for Schools

Name:

Class:

REVIEW (UNITS 1–3): WRITING AND SPEAKING

SPEAKING STUDENT A

Task 1
Ask your partner these questions.

- How old are you?
- Where do you live?

Task 2
Ask your partner these questions. Use the extra questions in brackets, if necessary.

Let's talk about **free time activities**.

- How much of your free time do you spend online? (Do you go online every evening?)
- What do you like doing online? (Do you chat online with your friends?)
- What hobbies do you like doing in your free time? (Do you like watching films?)

Now, tell me something about **your favourite website**.

- Why do you like this website?
- How often do you go on it?
- Do your friends like it too?

REVIEW (UNITS 1–3): WRITING AND SPEAKING

SPEAKING STUDENT B

Task 1
Ask your partner these questions.

- How old are you?
- Where do you live?

Task 2
Ask your partner these questions. Use the extra questions in brackets, if necessary.

Let's talk about **school**.

- How do you get to school and home again every day? (Do you walk to school and back?)
- Where do you usually do your homework? (Do you do your homework with a friend?)

Now, please tell me something about **your favourite day at school**.

- Which is your favourite lesson?
- Why do you like it?
- Do your friends like it too?

GOLD experience 2ND EDITION — A2 Key for Schools

Name: _____

Class: _____

REVIEW (UNITS 1–3): WRITING AND SPEAKING

TEACHER'S INSTRUCTIONS

Tell students (in pairs) that they will first ask and answer questions. Allocate students A or B and give them time to think of questions. A should ask B questions first. Let them begin by instructing them:

(*Candidate A*), please ask your questions to Candidate B.

(*Candidate B*), please answer the questions (use names). *Candidate B should answer the questions.*

Then, they should change.

(*Candidate B*), please ask your questions to Candidate A.

(*Candidate A*), please answer the questions.

Check that students are asking and answering questions and that communication is achieved (the question is understandable and the answer is appropriate).

At the end, thank the students and tell them they can leave.

GOLD experience 2ND EDITION A2

REVIEW (UNITS 4–6): LANGUAGE TEST A

VOCABULARY

Task 1
Complete the sentences with the correct words. Use the first letter to help you.

1 My dad and I often go **f**............................ by the river at the weekend.
2 The **s**............................ on my phone is very small so I prefer emailing from my laptop.
3 I wrote all the new vocabulary in my **n**............................ and then learned it in the evening.
4 Our **j**............................ to London was very long last night – almost five hours.
5 There was an amazing **m**............................ at the party and he found some playing cards in my shoe!
6 The new science-**f**............................ film is about the year 2080 and it's great.
7 Which **p**............................ does the Manchester train leave from?
8 These jeans were a **b**............................ in the new clothes shop – only £10!

[8]

Task 2
Choose the correct verb to complete the sentences.

9 We're going to **go / catch** the 6.30 train to Newcastle.
10 My sister learned to **drive / ride** a bike when she was five years old.
11 I always **wear / put** headphones when I listen to music on the train.
12 How much did you **spend / pay** for the concert tickets?
13 I'm in a band and we're going to **enter / perform** in a talent show next Saturday.
14 I think we'll **travel / take** by bus on our next trip to London.
15 The bus journey took longer than usual and I didn't **get / go** home until 4.30.

[7]

Task 3
Choose the correct answer (A, B or C).

16 Dan is waiting at the .... just outside his house.
  A tram B platform C bus stop
17 My brother loves telling funny stories and wants to be a ....
  A comedian B magician C guitarist
18 The .... to Italy was six hours and I watched two films.
  A travel B flight C ride
19 My mum loves .... music from the 17th century.
  A classical B animation C talent
20 Tom Hardy, the actor, is .... in the film. I really liked him.
  A kind B true C awesome
21 I didn't .... the jeans in the shop and they're the wrong size.
  A try on B wear C put
22 My English friend likes painting so I took her to see an art ....
  A museum B theatre C exhibition
23 Dad didn't have money with him, so he paid by ....
  A card B cash C pence
24 My cousin has a new boat and last weekend we .... across to the island.
  A sailed B rode C swam
25 Did you see that interesting .... about animals on TV last night?
  A concert B documentary C action film

[10]

GOLD experience 2ND EDITION A2 Key for Schools

Name: _____
Class: _____

REVIEW (UNITS 4–6): LANGUAGE TEST A

GRAMMAR

Task 1
Choose the correct option to complete the sentences.

26 **Do you walk / Are you walking** to school every morning?
27 **I'm always / I always am** tired on Saturday mornings.
28 I'm sorry I missed your call, but I **had / was having** a shower.
29 I **meet / am meeting** the head teacher in her office at 2.30.
30 This is the **busiest / most busy** shop in the shopping centre.

[ ] 5

Task 2
Complete the sentences with the correct form of the words in brackets.

31 We usually .... (go) to London by train, but today we .... (travel) by car.
32 Mark .... (arrange) the tennis matches last week and I .... (play) Malcolm tomorrow at 10.45.
33 My phone was .... (expensive) than yours, but Sarah's got .... (expensive) phone in the class.
34 I .... (wait) at the bus stop when it .... (start) to rain.
35 My sister .... (go) shopping with Maria yesterday, but she .... (not / buy) anything.

[ ] 10

Task 3
For each question write the correct answer. Write one word for each gap.

Hi Rose

Hello from Paris! We arrived on Monday and we **(36)** .... having an amazing time. I phoned you an hour **(37)** .... , but perhaps you **(37)** .... playing tennis?

The journey here was great. We didn't have **(38)** .... problems. After we arrived at Charles de Gaulle airport, we took a taxi to our hotel.

Yesterday, we went to a museum – there are so **(39)** .... museums in Paris! For me, **(40)** .... best one is

the Rodin Museum! Then we **(41)** .... shopping. What a shock! The shops in the Champs Elysees are more expensive **(42)** .... all the shops in London! Tomorrow, we're going **(43)** .... take a boat trip along the River Seine. I hope it's sunny!

I **(44)** .... be home on Wednesday. I can call you then.

Peter

[ ] 10

Total: [ ] 50

GOLD experience 2ND EDITION A2 Key for Schools

Name: _____
Class: _____

REVIEW (UNITS 4–6): LANGUAGE TEST B

VOCABULARY

Task 1
Complete the sentences with the correct words. Use the first letter to help you.

1 My brother doesn't like **r**............................ films where people fall in love!
2 We went on a **h**............................ trip over the mountains while we were in Switzerland.
3 There are three **g**............................ in our band and one singer.
4 It was a very **s**............................ film and I had bad dreams after watching it.
5 What was the **p**............................ of those shoes in the sale?
6 My friend's dad is a great **c**............................ and always makes us laugh!
7 There are twenty-eight **p**............................ in our class, and I don't know all their names yet.
8 I need to borrow some books from the **l**............................ before I do this homework.

[8]

Task 2
Choose the correct verb to complete the sentences.

9 We're going to **make / perform** the school play in the theatre in town.
10 My sister is too young to **drive / ride** a car.
11 I **cost / saved** a lot of money in the sales last week.
12 Can we **go / get** on foot to the museum or do you want to catch the bus?
13 My friend **did / made** a vlog while she was staying in the USA.
14 Last month we drove to visit my uncle in Scotland, but next time we'll **take / go** the train.
15 You can get the information for our project if you **visit / go** this website.

[7]

Task 3
Choose the correct answer (A, B or C).

16 The .... film was very clever and the characters looked like real people.
   A classical   B action   C animation
17 Our .... to school this morning took a very long time.
   A travelling   B journey   C travel
18 I prefer .... stories to fiction because I can learn a lot from them.
   A scary   B funny   C true
19 Did you find any .... in the shopping centre last weekend?
   A sales   B prices   C bargains
20 In the morning, the .... is always very busy, with lots of people travelling to work.
   A plane   B underground   C car
21 I hope you got a .... when you bought those shoes.
   A card   B cost   C receipt
22 The winner of the .... show was a rock singer.
   A documentary   B talent   C concert
23 It's good to .... to school, because it's healthier!
   A drive   B cycle   C ride
24 Every summer there's an open-air .... in the park.
   A theatre   B museum   C documentary
25 I .... my homework with my friend last night.
   A made   B took   C did

[10]

Photocopiable © Pearson Education Limited 2018

GOLD experience 2ND EDITION A2

REVIEW (UNITS 4–6): LANGUAGE TEST B

GRAMMAR

Task 1
Choose the correct option to complete the sentences.
26 My dad **usually cooks / cooks** usually dinner on Sundays.
27 This exercise is **more easy / easier** than exercise 3.
28 The play **finished / was finishing** at 10.30.
29 **Do you wait / Are you waiting** for Annie?
30 My brother **plays / is playing** in the football match at the weekend.

Task 2
Complete the sentences with the correct form of the words in brackets.
31 The boots are .... (cheap) online than in the department store, but the .... (cheap) ones are in the market.
32 Tina .... (love) pop music, but she .... (not / enjoy) rock.
33 I .... (do) did all my homework yesterday so this evening, I .... (relax) and watch TV for a few hours.
34 My dad .... (work) for a big international company in London, but at the moment he .... (work) in Paris.
35 My mum .... (cook) dinner when we suddenly .... (hear) a loud crash in the kitchen.

Task 3
For each question write the correct answer. Write one word for each gap.

Hi Ben,

Hello from London! I'm staying here for a week with my friend Allan. I arrived two days **(36)** .... London is busy and there are so **(37)** .... cars, but Allan lives next to a park and it's prettier **(38)** .... where I live! There aren't **(39)** .... parks near my home.

We went to **(40)** .... most expensive hotel in London for a meal yesterday. I'm not going **(41)** .... tell you the price! We **(42)** .... eating dinner when a girl came in. It was your favourite singer!

Tonight, Allan's parents **(43)** .... taking me to a show. They bought some cheap tickets **(44)** .... week.

(45) .... you be home later? I can call you about 11.30?

See you soon

Richard

GOLD experience
2ND EDITION

A2 Key for Schools

Name:
Class:

REVIEW (UNITS 4–6): WRITING AND SPEAKING

WRITING

Look at the three pictures. Write the story shown in the pictures.

Write **35 words** or more on a separate answer sheet.

GOLD experience
2ND EDITION — A2 Key for Schools

Name:

Class:

REVIEW (UNITS 4–6): WRITING AND SPEAKING

SPEAKING STUDENT A

Task 1
Look at some pictures that show different things to do in your free time.

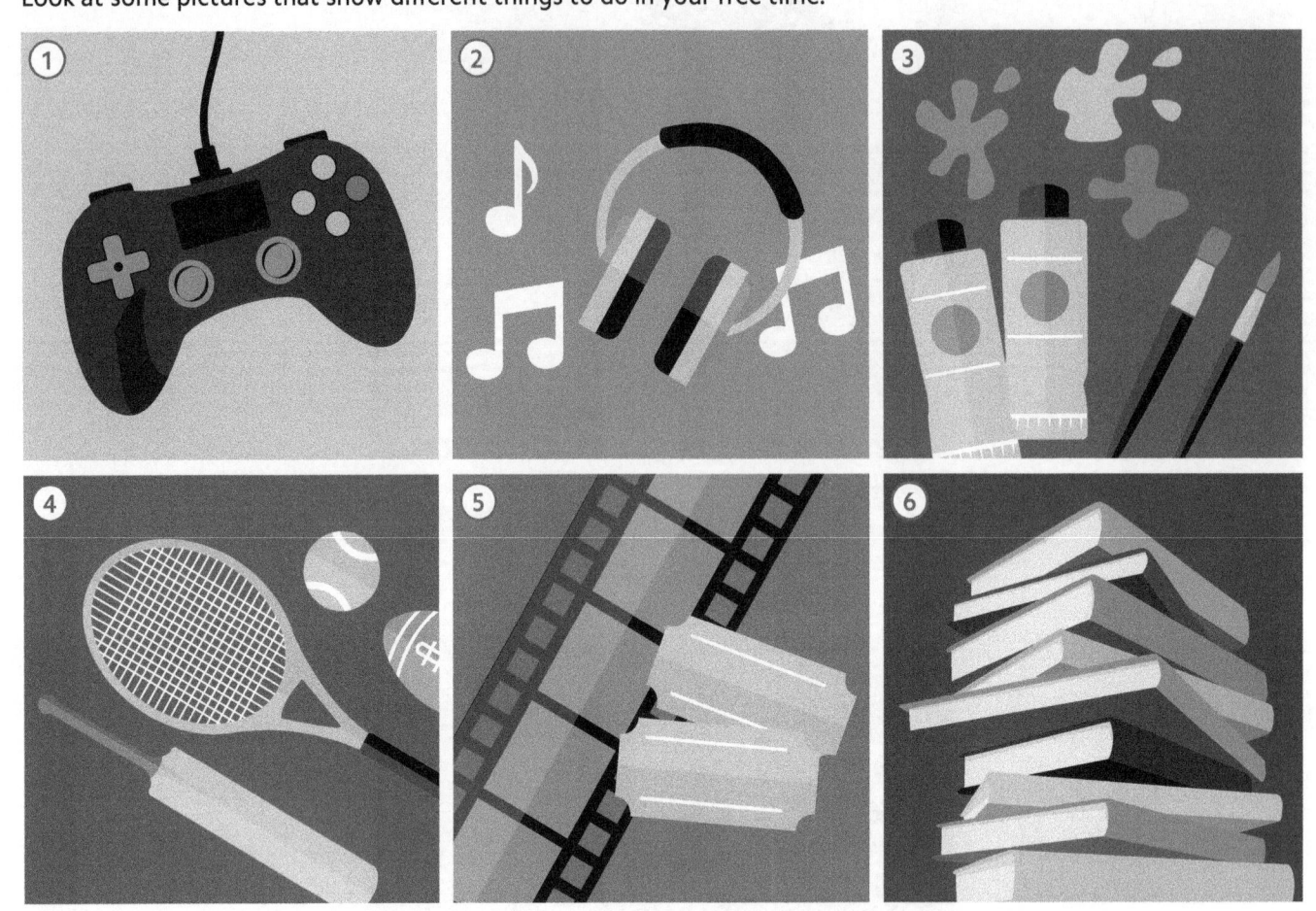

Task 2
Your teacher will ask you one or two questions about holidays.

REVIEW (UNITS 4–6): WRITING AND SPEAKING

SPEAKING STUDENT B

Task 1
Look at some pictures that show different things to do in your free time.

Task 2
Your teacher will ask you one or two questions about holidays.

REVIEW (UNITS 4–6): WRITING AND SPEAKING

TEACHER'S INSTRUCTIONS

Task 1

Tell students that they will discuss some pictures in pairs. Show them the pictures and say:

Here are some pictures that show different things to do in your free time.

Then, say: *Do you like these different things to do in your free time? Say why or why not. I'll say that again.*

Do you like these different things to do in your free time? Say why or why not.

All right? Now, talk together.

Allow students a minimum of 1 minute (maximum 2 minutes) to discuss the pictures. Then move on to Task 2.

Task 2

Ask Student B: *Do you prefer to go on holiday to a different country or stay in your own country? (Why?)*

Then ask Student A: *What about you? Do you prefer to go on holiday to a different country or stay in your own country? (Why?)*

Ask Student A: *Which place would you like to go to on holiday in the future? (Why?)*

Then ask Student B: *Which place would you like to go to on holiday in the future? (Why?)*

At the end, thank the students and tell them they can leave.

GOLD experience 2ND EDITION A2 Key for Schools

REVIEW (UNITS 7–9): LANGUAGE TEST A

VOCABULARY

Task 1
Complete the sentences with these words. There are two words you do not need to use.

> bee   equipment   healthy   island   knife
> lake   monkey   practice   sick   zero

1 Australia is a very large ....
2 The temperature fell below .... last night.
3 A .... is an insect that makes honey.
4 You can use this .... to cut the vegetables.
5 You'll feel .... if you don't stop eating those chocolates.
6 To be ...., you need to eat well and do enough exercise.
7 I think running is a great sport because you don't need lots of expensive ....
8 Have you got basketball .... this afternoon?

[8]

Task 2
Choose the correct word to complete the sentences.

9 Did you have / take a nice breakfast today?
10 Would you like to go to / for a walk this afternoon?
11 When you're cooking, it's important to follow the information / instructions carefully.
12 It's very dry / wet in the desert.
13 Do you enjoy going / doing gymnastics?
14 You should always wear a helmet / goggles when you go cycling.
15 If you want to play tennis, I can lend you a referee / racket.

[7]

Task 3
Choose the correct answer (A, B or C).

> Hi Alex
>
> I'm having a great **(16)** .... in Switzerland. We're staying in a nice hotel in the mountains. It's **(17)** .... hot here. Yesterday we **(18)** .... one of the mountains. It was hard work, but it was great when we got to the **(19)** .... It was nice and cool there and the **(20)** .... were amazing. Tomorrow we're going to go up another mountain, but we're going to go **(21)** .... train, not on **(22)** .... That'll be easier, but not as good **(23)** ....
>
> The food here is delicious and we eat outside every day. I think food tastes better in the **(24)** .... air! Yesterday, I had some really great pasta with chicken salad and a wonderful ice cream for **(25)** ....
>
> Hope you're having a good time too.
>
> See you soon.
>
> Sam

16 A travel   B holiday   C journey
17 A boiling   B frying   C freezing
18 A drove   B rode   C climbed
19 A bottom   B centre   C top
20 A views   B sights   C looks
21 A on   B to   C by
22 A leg   B foot   C body
23 A work   B fun   C time
24 A windy   B sunny   C fresh
25 A meal   B dessert   C starters

[10]

Photocopiable © Pearson Education Limited 2018   107

GOLD experience A2 2ND EDITION

REVIEW (UNITS 7–9): LANGUAGE TEST A

GRAMMAR

Task 1
Choose the correct word or phrase to complete the sentences.
26 Maria **could** / **couldn't** do gymnastics yesterday because she left her trainers at home.
27 Jose has **never** / **ever** seen snow.
28 Children under the age of eight **can't** / **don't have to** swim in the pool without an adult.
29 If you drink a glass of cold water, you **feel** / **will feel** better.
30 Dad and I will go for a long walk at the weekend, if the weather **is** / **will** be nice.

[10]

Task 2
Complete the sentences with the correct form of the words in brackets.
31 If I .... (see) any nice trainers tomorrow, I .... (buy) them, for sure.
32 .... (you / ever / sleep) in a tent?
33 I .... (have) sushi if I .... (go) to the Japanese restaurant tonight. I love sushi.
34 My little brother .... (never / be) in a plane.
35 .... (you eat) today? You look hungry.

[7]

Task 3
Complete the text. Write one word in each gap.

Learning to play a new sport can **(36)** .... difficult. My brother joined a table tennis club three months **(37)** .... and the coach told him, 'You will need to practise a lot **(38)** .... you want to become a good player.'

He really wanted to get on the team, so he **(39)** .... to the club every day after school. Now, he **(40)** .... play quite well.

The coach now says he plays much **(41)** .... than most of the other people who go to the club. So he's on the team now and next Saturday he **(42)** .... play in his first big competition.

I **(43)** .... going to see him play, and I hope he wins!

[8]

Total: [50]

108 Photocopiable © Pearson Education Limited 2018

GOLD experience 2ND EDITION — A2 Key for Schools

REVIEW (UNITS 7–9): LANGUAGE TEST B

VOCABULARY

Task 1
Complete the sentences with these words. There are two words you do not need to use.

equipment   healthy   islands   knife   lake
monkeys   practice   referee   sick   spoon

1 Dan spent the day in bed because he felt ....
2 You can use this .... to eat your dessert.
3 What time does football .... start today?
4 Greenland is one of the largest .... in the world.
5 Bella does a lot of sport because she wants to stay ....
6 The .... stopped the match and asked the player to leave.
7 I like fishing by the .... There are lots of fish there.
8 There's a new shop in town that sells all sorts of sports ....

[8]

Task 2
Choose the correct word to complete the sentences.

9 Could I borrow your badminton racket / goggles?
10 My family loves frying / grilling food on the barbecue in summer.
11 You must wear a helmet / cap on a motorbike.
12 What did you have / take for dinner yesterday?
13 It's freezing / boiling hot in this room. Open the window!
14 When do you go / find time to relax?
15 Do you enjoy going / doing cycling?

[7]

Task 3
Choose the correct answer (A, B or C).

Hi Amanda

I'm on **(16)** .... in the north of Sweden with my grandparents. I'm having a great time. There's lots of snow and it's **(17)** .... cold. Yesterday we all **(18)** .... skiing – cross-country skiing not mountain skiing. It's hard work, but it's good **(19)** ....

We're staying in a lovely hotel in the forest. My room has a beautiful **(20)** .... of a lake. We're all sleeping very **(21)** .... because we're spending all our time in the fresh **(22)** ....

The **(23)** .... here is delicious. We **(24)** .... a good breakfast every day, and the cook in the hotel **(25)** .... the most fantastic bread and cakes.

See you soon.

Katy

16	A travel	B trip	C holiday
17	A boiling	B frying	C freezing
18	A played	B went	C got
19	A fun	B place	C game
20	A sight	B view	C look
21	A good	B better	C well
22	A fresh	B windy	C sunny
23	A meal	B food	C dish
24	A do	B make	C have
25	A bakes	B grills	C fries

[10]

GOLD experience 2ND EDITION A2 Key for Schools

REVIEW (UNITS 7–9): LANGUAGE TEST B

GRAMMAR

Task 1
Choose the correct word or phrase to complete the sentences.

26 If it **is / will** be sunny tomorrow, we'll go to the beach.
27 You **can't / don't** have to go skiing if you don't want to.
28 Pat **could / couldn't** already ski a little when he was only five.
29 If I help you with your maths homework, **do / will** you help me with the history?
30 What is the best film you have **ever / never** seen?

10

Task 2
Complete the sentences with the correct form of the words in brackets.

31 ………………… (you / ever / eat) sushi?
32 If grandpa ………………… (give) me some money for my birthday, I ………………… (get) a new cycle helmet.
33 Kim ………………… (never / go) to Paris, but she would like to go.
34 Mum ………………… (drive) you home, if you ………………… (come) to my house tonight.
35 I ………………… (not / drink) anything all day, and now I'm really thirsty.

7

Task 3
Complete the text. Write one word in each gap.

My class started learning to play hockey **(36)** ………………… year. At first it was very difficult for me. I **(37)** ………………… play well, but our teacher was very good and soon I was much **(38)** ………………… at the game and now I really enjoy it.

My friends and I now play every day after school. Our teacher says that we **(39)** ………………… soon be in the school hockey team **(40)** ………………… we try hard. I'm sure we **(41)** ………………… stop. We all love the game too much.

Tonight, my friends and I **(42)** ………………… going to practise. We **(43)** ………………… want to do anything else!

8

Total: 50

GOLD experience
2ND EDITION

A2 Key for Schools

Name:
Class:

REVIEW (UNITS 7–9): WRITING AND SPEAKING

WRITING
Look at the three pictures. Write the story shown in the pictures.

Write **35 words** or more on a separate answer sheet.

GOLD experience
2ND EDITION A2 Key for Schools

REVIEW (UNITS 7-9): WRITING AND SPEAKING

SPEAKING STUDENT A

Task 1
Look at some pictures that show different weekend activities.

Task 2
Your teacher will ask you one or two questions about weekend activities.

GOLD experience
2ND EDITION **A2** Key for Schools

Name:
Class:

REVIEW (UNITS 7–9): WRITING AND SPEAKING

SPEAKING STUDENT B

Task 1
Look at some pictures that show different weekend activities.

Task 2
Your teacher will ask you one or two questions about weekend activities.

GOLD experience 2ND EDITION — A2 Key for Schools

Name: _____

Class: _____

REVIEW (UNITS 7–9): WRITING AND SPEAKING

TEACHER'S INSTRUCTIONS

Task 1

Tell students that they will discuss some pictures in pairs. Show them the pictures and say:

Here are some pictures that show different weekend activities.

Then, say: *Do you like these different weekend activities? Say why or why not. I'll say that again.*

Do you like these different weekend activities? Say why or why not.

All right? Now, talk together.

Allow students a minimum of 1 minute (maximum 2 minutes) to discuss the pictures. Then move on to Task 2.

Task 2

Ask Student B: *Do you prefer doing the same thing every weekend or doing different things? (Why?)*

Then ask Student A: *What about you? Do you prefer doing the same thing every weekend or doing different things (Why?)*

Ask Student A: *Do you prefer being at home, or doing sport? (Why?)*

Then ask Student B: *Do you prefer being at home, or doing sport? (Why?)*

At the end, thank the students and tell them they can leave.

GOLD experience
2ND EDITION A2 Key for Schools

Name: _____

Class: _____

END OF YEAR TEST A

LISTENING

You will hear a teacher talking to a class about a trip. You will hear the recording twice.

Task 1
Choose the correct answer (A, B or C).

1 Which sport did Natasha enjoy most?

A   B   C

2 What was the weather like at the weekend?

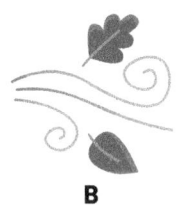

A   B   C

3 What is Dad going to make?

A   B   C

4 Which girl is the boy's sister?

A   B   C

5 What does the boy need to borrow?

A   B   C

[10]

Task 2
Complete the information. Write one word, or a number, or a date, or a time.

Class Trip for Boys	
Day of trip:	Monday
Name of teacher:	Mrs **(6)** ....
Going to:	**(7)** .... Museum
Going by:	**(8)** ....
Place to meet:	playground
Time to meet:	**(9)** ....
At the end of the visit there will be a **(10)**	

[5]

Photocopiable © Pearson Education Limited 2018   115

GOLD experience 2ND EDITION — A2 Key for Schools

END OF YEAR TEST A

LANGUAGE

Task 1
Choose the correct answer (A, B or C).

I'm **(11)** .... the New Forest in the south of England soon. I want to see the National Motor Museum. It's in a beautiful village by a **(12)** ...., in the middle of a forest. The Museum is more than sixty-five years old, and it's the **(13)** .... in the area. There are some amazing cars to see. You won't **(14)** .... bored! The Museum is in the gardens of a lovely old house, and visitors can go round many of the rooms. The guides **(15)** .... clothes from when the house was built. It's really interesting. And of course, there are shops which **(16)** .... books about the cars and other souvenirs. I'll go there **(17)** .... train or I might drive – it's a great journey through the forest.

It's easy to get information about the museum. Just go online and **(18)** .... the brochure!

11	A going	B travelling	C visiting
12	A river	B sea	C coast
13	A popular	B most popular	C more popular
14	A get	B go	C make
15	A put	B try on	C wear
16	A cost	B sell	C pay
17	A to	B by	C on
18	A click	B visit	C download

8

Task 2
Complete the text. Write one word in each gap.

Hi Alan,

I hope you **(19)** .... well! Everything is OK here. I **(20)** .... thinking about you yesterday. We had an English test, and I remembered you had your end of term tests a week **(21)** .... I hope that they **(22)** .... easy.

Are you going **(23)** .... study any new subjects next term? We've got a new Maths teacher and I hope I get better marks **(24)** .... I got last term!

(25) .... you done anything interesting recently? Write soon and let me know!

Love,

Sandra

7

GOLD experience 2ND EDITION — A2 Key for Schools

Name: _____
Class: _____

END OF YEAR TEST A

READING

Read the text and answer the questions.

Great holidays!

Three readers write about their holidays.

A Jade

I like beach holidays and my favourite place is Saint Lucia. It's an island in the Caribbean. My parents took me and my brother there two years ago and then again last year. It was great because everyone speaks English! The food was brilliant, especially the fish, and the beaches were clean with not many people! It was a bit too hot for me, but it was better than rain! I still email a girl called Penny who was in the same hotel as we were. One day, we're both going to go back.

B Ellie

A few months ago I went to an English town called Lyme Regis for a three day school trip. It's got a beach where you can find very old rocks. I bought a very old and pretty one in a shop. There's also a rock museum there, which we went to. We only had one sunny day and we ate fish and chips by the sea! It was fun, but afterwards I didn't feel very well! I'd like to go again, but if I do, I won't eat fish! And next time I'd like to stay in a hotel, not in a tent.

C Judy

I first went to France with my school when I was eleven and it was amazing. It was cool to speak to the people in French! Last year I went again and stayed with my French friend. She lives in a small town by the sea. It's usually very quiet, but there were a lot of people. It was sunny and warm all the time, which I loved. Just before we came home I fell down some steps and broke my arm. I hope I can go back next year, maybe with my family, but I'll be more careful!

Task 1

Choose the correct answer (A, B or C).

Which person:

	Jade	Ellie	Judy
26 met a new friend on holiday?	A	B	C
27 went camping?	A	B	C
28 went somewhere that wasn't crowded?	A	B	C
29 had an accident while on holiday?	A	B	C
30 went on a recent holiday with her school?	A	B	C

[10]

GOLD experience 2ND EDITION A2 Key for Schools

Name: _____

Class: _____

END OF YEAR TEST A

Beth Newbold, winner of the junior chef competition, writes about learning to cook.

I was quite young, about five when I made my first cake, I think. And it wasn't my mum or dad who taught me. My parents didn't cook much. Mum didn't enjoy it, perhaps because she had a busy life. And dad – well – his meals were terrible! So, we usually ate things like burgers or pasta and boiled vegetables or chips from the shop!

I only ate well when we went to my gran's. She was a great cook and I loved the smell of her kitchen. She made fresh cakes and bread and biscuits. Her soups were amazing too. She showed me how to bake cakes. I was short at that time and I remember I had to stand on a chair to work on her table!

Making my first cake was really exciting. I mixed it with my gran's 'magic' spoon! It tasted very good to me because I cooked it (with a little help from gran). I think it was probably horrible, but gran said it was excellent! Then I regularly helped with the meals at gran's. I watched her carefully and she gave me a lot of her secrets about cooking. She never used recipe books!

Then gran found an advertisement for the TV competition in a magazine at her hairdresser's and she sent them my name! She didn't even tell my mum. When I heard, I was really angry. I get nervous about competitions because I don't like losing! But gran told me I was a great cook and she was proud of me. So, I took part in the competition. I couldn't believe it when I won a course of cooking lessons with a top chef!

Task 2

Choose the correct answer (A, B or C).

31 What does Beth say about her dad?
  A He often went to restaurants.
  B he cooked badly.
  C He was always busy.

32 What does Beth remember about the kitchen table?
  A She had a problem reaching it.
  B She sat there to watch her grandmother cook.
  C She did her homework on it.

33 Beth now thinks her first cake was
  A excellent
  B worse that she thought at the time
  C made by her gran

34 Who wrote in to the competition?
  A Beth.
  B Beth's mum.
  C Beth's gran.

35 Why was Beth angry about the competition at first?
  A She thought she was a bad cook.
  B Her gran didn't tell her mother about it.
  C She thought she might not win.

GOLD experience
2ND EDITION — A2 Key for Schools

Name: _____
Class: _____

END OF YEAR TEST B

LISTENING

You will hear a teacher talking to a class about a trip. You will hear the recording twice.

Task 1
Choose the correct answer (A, B or C).

1 Which sport did Josh enjoy most?

   A    B    C

2 What is the weather like today?

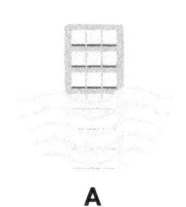

   A    B    C

3 What is the girl going to make?

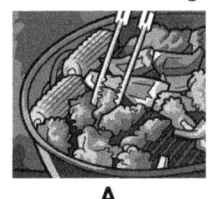

   A    B    C

4 Which girl is the boy's cousin?

   A    B    C

5 What does the boy not need today?

   A   B    C

[10]

Task 2
Complete the information. Write one word, or a number, or a date, or a time.

Class Trip for Girls

Day of trip: Monday

Name of teacher: Mrs **(6)** ....

Going to: **(7)** .... Museum

Going by: **(8)** ....

Place to meet: School hall

Time to meet: **(9)** ....

At the end of the visit there will be a **(10)** ....

[5]

Photocopiable © Pearson Education Limited 2018

GOLD experience
2ND EDITION — A2 Key for Schools

END OF YEAR TEST B

LANGUAGE

Task 1
Choose the correct answer (A, B or C).

Have you ever **(11)** .... to the New Forest in the south of England? No? Then you must go there! There's a beautiful village **(12)** .... Beaulieu and there you can go to the National Motor **(13)** .... It's amazing. It **(14)** .... over sixty-five years ago with only five cars and now there are **(15)** .... than 250! It's **(16)** .... to a very old and beautiful house, Palace House, where a very old English family, the Montagues, live. Visitors can go round the house and see the old rooms and furniture. You can get to Beaulieu **(17)** .... car and it's only a ten-minute bus ride from the nearest railway station. **(18)** .... the website and read about it. You'll have a great day!

11	A seen	B been	C visited
12	A called	B name	C signed
13	A exhibition	B museum	C department
14	A became	B arrived	C started
15	A more	B most	C many
16	A beside	B in front	C next
17	A on	B by	C in
18	A Visit	B Go	C Click

[8]

Task 2
Complete the text. Write one word in each gap.

How **(19)** .... you? I **(20)** .... seen you for a long time! I'm fine – busy as usual. **(21)** .... you get good grades in your end of term tests last month?

It's the start of a new term and I **(22)** .... studying a new language – Italian! When I went to Rome with my parents **(23)** .... year, I **(24)** .... say anything in Italian. Now I can have a simple conversation! We're going **(25)** .... visit Italy again in July and I hope I can say even more.

Write soon!

[7]

120   Photocopiable © Pearson Education Limited 2018

GOLD experience 2ND EDITION — A2 Key for Schools

Name: _____

Class: _____

END OF YEAR TEST B

READING

Read the text and answer the questions.

Great holidays!

Three readers write about their holidays.

Jade

I love going on holiday, and my favourite place is Barbados. It's an island in the Caribbean. My parents took me and my brother there last year. The food was brilliant, and the beaches were clean with not many people! It was a bit too hot for me, but it was better than rain! I remember my lovely holiday there when I have a cup of tea every day, because I have it in a mug with Barbados on it!

Ellie

A few years ago I went with my school to a town called Lyme Regis for three days. It's got a beach where you can find very old rocks. I bought a very old and pretty one in a shop. There's also a museum there, which we went to. We only had one sunny day and we ate fish and chips by the sea! It was fun. Just before we came home I fell down some steps and broke my arm. I'd like to go again, but if I do, I'll be careful! I still email a boy called Ben, who was at the same hotel. He was there on a school trip too.

Judy

I first went to France with my school when I was eleven and it was amazing. It was cool to speak to the people in French! Last year I went again with my friend and her mum and dad and we stayed in a little hotel by the sea. It was sunny and warm all the time, which I loved. One evening we went to a sea food restaurant and I felt very sick afterwards! I hope I can go back next year, maybe with my family, but I won't eat fish!

Task 1

Choose the correct answer (A, B or C).

Which person:

	Jade	Ellie	Judy
26 regularly uses something she got on holiday?	A	B	C
27 had an accident while she was on holiday?	A	B	C
28 enjoyed the weather on her holiday?	A	B	C
29 went on holiday with her family?	A	B	C
30 had a problem with some food?	A	B	C

10

GOLD experience 2ND EDITION — A2 Key for Schools

END OF YEAR TEST B

> **Beth Newbold, winner of the junior chef competition, writes about learning to cook.**
>
> I was quite young, about five when I made my first cake, I think. And it wasn't my mum or dad who taught me. My parents didn't cook much. Mum didn't enjoy it, perhaps because she had a busy life. And dad – well – his meals were terrible! So, we usually ate things which were easy to cook, like burgers or pasta and boiled vegetables!
>
> I only ate well when we went to my gran's. She was a great cook and I loved the smell of her kitchen. She made fresh cakes and bread and biscuits. Her soups were amazing too. She showed me how to bake cakes. I was short at that time and I remember – I had to stand on a chair to work on her table!
>
> Making my first cake was really exciting. I mixed it with my gran's 'magic' spoon! It tasted very good to me because I cooked it (with a little help from gran). It was probably horrible, but gran said it was excellent! Then I regularly helped with the meals at gran's. I watched her carefully and she gave me a lot of her secrets about cooking – she never used recipe books!
>
> Then gran found an advertisement for the TV competition in a magazine at her hairdresser's and she sent them my name! She didn't even tell my mum. When I heard, I was really angry. I get nervous in competitions because I don't like losing! But gran told me I was a great cook and she was proud of me. So, I did the competition. I couldn't believe it when I won a course of cooking lessons with a top chef!

Task 2

Choose the correct answer (A, B or C).

31 What does Beth say about her parents?
   A They were good cooks.
   B They cooked a lot.
   C They made simple meals.

32 What was true about Beth's grandmother?
   A She bought her a lot of cakes.
   B She taught her to cook.
   C She always served soup.

33 Beth's grandmother gave her
   A an old recipe book.
   B a favourite spoon.
   C some special advice.

34 How did Beth's grandmother learn about the competition?
   A She saw it on TV.
   B She read about it.
   C She heard about from her hairdresser.

35 Beth agreed to enter the competition because
   A her gran encouraged her.
   B she was sure she could win.
   C she wanted to win the prize.

END OF YEAR TEST: WRITING

WRITING

Task 1

You want to invite your English friend, Alex, to visit you next year.
Write an email to Alex.

> In your email:
>
> - ask Alex to visit you
>
> - say when is the best time to come
>
> - say what you can do together

Write **25 words** or more on a separate answer sheet.

Task 2

Look at the three pictures. Write the story shown in the pictures.

Write **35 words** or more on a separate answer sheet.

GOLD experience 2ND EDITION — A2 Key for Schools

Name:
Class:

END OF YEAR TEST: SPEAKING

SPEAKING STUDENT A

Task 1

Ask your partner these questions.

> Let's talk about **sport**.
>
> - How often do you do sport?
>
> - Who do you do sport with?
>
> - When did you last do some sport?
>
> Now, tell me something about **your favourite sport.**

Task 2

Look at some pictures where people often spend time.
Do you like spending time in these places? Say why or why not?
Which of these places do you like best?

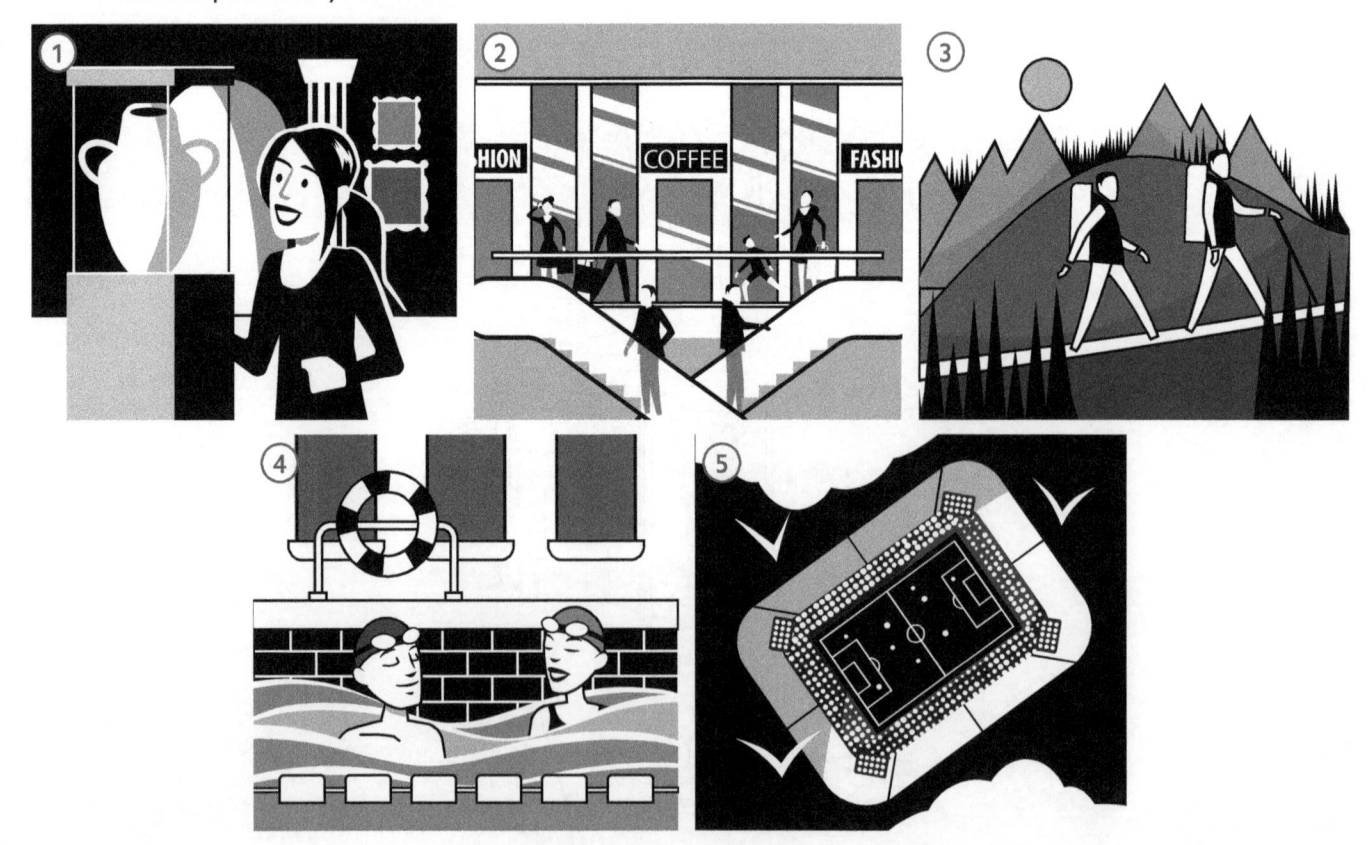

124

Photocopiable © Pearson Education Limited 2018

END OF YEAR TEST: SPEAKING

SPEAKING STUDENT B

Task 1
Ask your partner these questions.

> Let's talk about **films**.
>
> - Where do you usually watch films?
>
> - Which film would you like to see next?
>
> - What kind of films do you like most?
>
> Now, tell me something about **the best film you've ever seen**.

Task 2
Here are some pictures where people often spend time.
Do you like spending time in these places? Say why or why not?
Which of these places do you like best?

GOLD experience
2ND EDITION A2 Key for Schools

Name: _____

Class: _____

END OF YEAR TEST: SPEAKING

TEACHER'S INSTRUCTIONS

Task 1

Tell students that they will first ask and answer questions in pairs. Allocate students A or B and give them time to think of questions. A should ask B questions first. Let them begin by instructing them:

(*Candidate A*), please ask your questions to Candidate B.

(*Candidate B*), please answer the questions (use names). *Candidate B should answer the questions.*

Then, they should change.

(*Candidate B*), please ask your questions to Candidate A.

(*Candidate A*), please answer the questions.

Check that students are asking and answering questions and that communication is achieved (the question is understandable and the answer is appropriate).

Task 2

Tell students that they will discuss some pictures in pairs. Show them the pictures and say:

Here are some pictures that show where people often spend time.

Then, say: *Do you like spending time in these places? Say why or why not. I'll say that again. Do you like spending time in these places? Say why or why not.*

All right? Now, talk together.

Allow students a minimum of 1 minute (maximum 2 minutes) to discuss the pictures. Then ask them to discuss this question: *Which of these places do you like best?*

Allow students about 1 minute to discuss this.

At the end, thank the students and tell them they can leave.

TEST ANSWER KEYS

GOLD experience 2ND EDITION **A2**

Diagnostic Test A

No	Key	Language Area
1	D	there is/there are
2	C	there is/there are (+ some/any)
3	C	vocabulary: everyday activities
4	B	present continuous
5	B	continuous form
6	A	present continuous
7	B	past simple
8	C	vocabulary: things we do
9	C	present simple
10	C	modal verbs: *must*
11	A	vocabulary: the weather
12	C	past simple
13	B	vocabulary: irregular verbs
14	C	comparative adjectives
15	D	superlative adjectives
16	A	vocabulary: clothes
17	C	vocabulary: *play, go* and *do*
18	B	*be going to*
19	C	*have got*
20	A	vocabulary: parts of the body
21	D	vocabulary: jobs
22	B	vocabulary: food and drink
23	A	vocabulary: adjectives to describe things
24	C	vocabulary: places in a town
25	C	imperatives
26	A	present simple and present continuous
27	B	present simple and present continuous
28	D	present simple and present continuous
29	B	present simple and present continuous
30	D	past simple and past continuous
31	C	past simple and past continuous
32	B	past simple and past continuous
33	D	past simple and past continuous
34	A	present perfect
35	B	present perfect
36	A	present perfect
37	C	present perfect
38	C	future forms
39	B	future forms
40	D	future forms
41	B	future forms
42	B	first conditional
43	D	first conditional
44	C	first conditional
45	D	comparatives and superlatives
46	B	comparatives and superlatives
47	A	comparatives and superlatives
48	D	*some/any, much/many*
49	C	*some/any, much/many*
50	A	*some/any, much/many*
51	B	*some/any, much/many*
52	B	*can* and *have to*
53	C	*can* and *have to*
54	A	*can* and *have to*
55	C	*can* and *have to*
56	D	*should*
57	B	*should*
58	B	*should*
59	B	vocabulary: free time activities
60	C	vocabulary: entertainment
61	D	vocabulary: weather
62	A	vocabulary: sport
63	C	vocabulary: travel
64	B	vocabulary: sport
65	C	vocabulary: entertainment
66	A	vocabulary: free time activities
67	D	vocabulary: travel
68	D	vocabulary: free time activities
69	B	vocabulary: travel
70	A	vocabulary: health
71	C	vocabulary: feelings
72	D	vocabulary: free time activities
73	A	vocabulary: sport
74	B	vocabulary: free time activities
75	D	vocabulary: travel
76	C	verb forms
77	D	verb forms
78	D	verb forms
79	B	*have to/must*
80	B	frequency adverbs
81	C	prepositions
82	A	prepositions
83	C	prepositions
84	A	prepositions
85	C	adjectives and adverbs
86	C	adjectives and adverbs
87	B	adjectives and adverbs
88	A	adjectives and adverbs
89	C	adjectives and adverbs
90	D	collocations
91	A	collocations
92	B	collocations
93	D	collocations
94	C	collocations
95	D	vocabulary: travel
96	B	vocabulary: places
97	C	vocabulary: places
98	A	vocabulary: education
99	B	vocabulary: travel
100	B	vocabulary: clothes

Placement Guidance:

- If students score fewer than 10 correct answers, consider starting in the level below.
- If students score between 10 and 40, start at the expected level and assess scores to check whether remediation is required.
- If students score between 50 to 75, assess scores and consider an additional oral interview to decide whether the expected level or the next level with some remediation would be more appropriate.
- Students who scored 75+ should be started at the next level.

Diagnostic Test B

No	Key	Language Area
1	C	there is/there are
2	D	vocabulary: days of the week
3	C	vocabulary: everyday activities
4	B	present continuous
5	C	continuous form
6	C	present continuous
7	D	past simple
8	C	vocabulary: things we do
9	A	present simple
10	B	modal verbs: must
11	C	vocabulary: the weather
12	A	past simple
13	B	vocabulary: irregular verbs
14	B	comparative adjectives
15	B	superlative adjectives
16	A	vocabulary: clothes
17	A	vocabulary: play, go and do
18	B	be going to
19	B	have got
20	C	vocabulary: parts of the body
21	C	vocabulary: jobs
22	C	vocabulary: food and drink
23	A	vocabulary: adjectives to describe things
24	B	vocabulary: places in a town
25	C	imperatives
26	D	present simple and present continuous
27	A	present simple and present continuous
28	C	present simple and present continuous
29	B	present simple and present continuous
30	B	past simple and past continuous
31	B	past simple and past continuous
32	A	past simple and past continuous
33	C	past simple and past continuous
34	A	present perfect
35	B	present perfect
36	C	present perfect
37	D	present perfect
38	B	future forms
39	B	future forms
40	D	future forms
41	A	future forms
42	B	first conditional
43	B	first conditional
44	C	first conditional
45	C	comparatives and superlatives
46	C	comparatives and superlatives
47	A	comparatives and superlatives
48	C	some/any, much/many
49	D	some/any, much/many
50	C	some/any, much/many
51	B	some/any, much/many
52	B	can and have to
53	A	can and have to
54	C	can and have to
55	D	can and have to
56	B	should
57	D	should
58	B	should
59	A	vocabulary: entertainment
60	D	vocabulary: sport
61	B	vocabulary: travel
62	B	vocabulary: weather
63	C	vocabulary: free time activities
64	B	vocabulary: travel
65	C	vocabulary: free time activities
66	C	vocabulary: shopping
67	D	vocabulary: entertainment
68	A	vocabulary: travel
69	B	vocabulary: health
70	B	vocabulary: free time activities
71	B	vocabulary: sport
72	C	vocabulary: feelings
73	A	vocabulary: free time activities
74	B	vocabulary: travel
75	C	vocabulary: free time activities
76	C	verb forms
77	D	frequency adverbs
78	C	have to/must
79	B	verb forms
80	B	verb forms
81	A	prepositions
82	B	prepositions
83	D	prepositions
84	B	prepositions
85	B	adjectives and adverbs
86	D	adjectives and adverbs
87	B	adjectives and adverbs
88	D	adjectives and adverbs
89	B	adjectives and adverbs
90	B	collocations
91	C	collocations
92	C	collocations
93	C	collocations
94	A	collocations
95	D	vocabulary: places
96	B	vocabulary: places
97	C	vocabulary: clothes
98	C	vocabulary: travel
99	A	vocabulary: places
100	B	vocabulary: education

Placement Guidance:

- If students score fewer than 10 correct answers, consider starting in the level below.
- If students score between 10 and 40, start at the expected level and assess scores to check whether remediation is required.
- If students score between 50 to 75, assess scores and consider an additional oral interview to decide whether the expected level or the next level with some remediation would be more appropriate.
- Students who scored 75+ should be started at the next level.

TEST ANSWER KEYS

GOLD experience 2ND EDITION A2

UNIT 1
LANGUAGE TEST A

Vocabulary

TASK 1

1 baking **2** fishing **3** painting **4** singing
For revision, go to Student's Book: p16

TASK 2

5 singing **6** fishing **7** baking **8** painting
For revision, go to Student's Book: p16

TASK 3

9 F **10** A **11** D **12** E **13** G **14** B **15** C
For revision, go to Student's Book: p16

TASK 4

16 C **17** B **18** C **19** C **20** B **21** A **22** B **23** C
24 A **25** C
For revision, go to Student's Book: p16, 17

Grammar

TASK 1

26 don't want **27** Do you go **28** speaks
29 doesn't do **30** often watches **31** doesn't like
32 does your mum go **33** Does your brother win
34 don't play **35** Do you want
For revision, go to Student's Book: p14

TASK 2

36 many **37** much **38** much **39** many **40** much
For revision, go to Student's Book: p16

TASK 3

41 She always feels nervous before a competition.
42 Paul never takes photos with his camera.
43 I am not often late for school.
44 Anna usually speaks quietly.
45 I don't always drink coffee for breakfast.
For revision, go to Student's Book: p14

LANGUAGE TEST B

Vocabulary

TASK 1

1 drawing **2** reading **3** dancing **4** camping
For revision, go to Student's Book: p16

TASK 2

5 reading **6** camping **7** drawing **8** dancing
For revision, go to Student's Book: p16

TASK 3

9 E **10** A **11** B **12** G **13** F **14** C **15** D
For revision, go to Student's Book: p16

TASK 4

16 C **17** B **18** A **19** B **20** A **21** B **22** C **23** A
24 C **25** A
For revision, go to Student's Book: p16, 17

Grammar

TASK 1

26 play **27** doesn't want **28** often enjoy
29 do you like **30** Does your dad work **31** don't collect
32 does your best friend live **33** doesn't bake
34 watches **35** Do your friends like
For revision, go to Student's Book: p14

TASK 2

36 many **37** much **38** much **39** many **40** much
For revision, go to Student's Book: p16

TASK 3

41 It is always hot in summer.
42 We never go to school on Saturday.
43 Marie sometimes goes swimming after school.
44 My dad doesn't often drive to work.
45 I'm usually early for lessons.
For revision, go to Student's Book: p14

SKILLS TEST A

Dictation

My friend has many interesting hobbies. She enjoys collecting postcards and sometimes goes fishing with her dad. I think that is awesome.

Listening

TASK 1

1 Saturday **2** 10.30 / ten thirty **3** Edwards
4 02779 381 420 **5** 50

TASK 2

6 exciting **7** students **8** 4 / four o'clock **9** dancing
10 £100

Reading

TASK 1

11 C **12** B **13** A **14** C **15** A **16** B **17** C

TASK 2

18 He loves his car. He likes cleaning, repairing and talking to it.
19 He likes playing the guitar and being in a band.
20 She likes spending money and going shopping.

TEST ANSWER KEYS

GOLD experience 2ND EDITION **A2**

SKILLS TEST B

Dictation
My friend has many interesting hobbies. She enjoys collecting postcards and sometimes goes fishing with her dad. I think that is awesome.

Listening
TASK 1
1 Thursday **2** 4 / four **3** (the) hall **4** Barnet **5** 100
TASK 2
6 news **7** Saturday **8** 10.30 / ten thirty **9** good **10** £50

Reading
TASK 1
11 C **12** A **13** B **14** A **15** B **16** C **17** B
TASK 2
18 He likes cooking and learning about meals from different countries.
19 She likes learning languages and going to Italian classes.
20 She likes being with her dogs and training them.

UNIT 2

LANGUAGE TEST A

Vocabulary
TASK 1
1 screen **2** webcam **3** mouse **4** keyboard **5** speakers **6** printer **7** digital camera **8** mobile phone
For revision, go to Student's Book: p27
TASK 2
9 an email **10** films **11** Click **12** download **13** have **14** chat **15** visit
For revision, go to Student's Book: p27
TASK 3
16 B **17** A **18** B **19** A **20** C **21** C **22** B **23** A **24** B **25** C
For revision, go to Student's Book: p27, p29, p31

Grammar
TASK 1
26 lying **27** typing **28** chatting **29** messaging **30** streaming
For revision, go to Student's Book: p26
TASK 2
31 Is he lying **32** are you typing **33** isn't messaging **34** 'm streaming **35** aren't chatting
For revision, go to Student's Book: p26

TASK 3
36 isn't **37** are **38** 'm not **39** are **40** is
For revision, go to Student's Book: p26
TASK 4
41 'm sitting **42** don't watch **43** is your brother doing **44** 'musing **45** Do you want
For revision, go to Student's Book: p28

LANGUAGE TEST B

Vocabulary
TASK 1
1 webcam **2** mobile phone **3** keyboard **4** headphones **5** laptop **6** printer **7** digital camera **8** screen
For revision, go to Student's Book: p27
TASK 2
9 video **10** stream **11** website **12** my friends **13** online **14** email **15** link
For revision, go to Student's Book: p27
TASK 3
16 C **17** B **18** C **19** A **20** C **21** A **22** B **23** C **24** A **25** A
For revision, go to Student's Book: p27, p29, p31

Grammar
TASK 1
26 giving **27** sending **28** sitting **29** writing **30** starting
For revision, go to Student's Book: p26
TASK 2
31 Are you writing **32** isn't giving **33** 're sitting **34** 's lying **35** Is this computer sending
For revision, go to Student's Book: p26
TASK 3
36 'm trying **37** works **38** are you buying **39** isn't working **40** is using
For revision, go to Student's Book: p26
TASK 4
41 aren't **42** is **43** 'm not **44** are **45** am
For revision, go to Student's Book: p28

TEST ANSWER KEYS

GOLD experience 2ND EDITION **A2**

SKILLS TEST A

Dictation

My friend has got an old mobile phone and it hasn't got any apps. The screen isn't big, but my friend can go online, send messages and stream music and films.

Listening

TASK 1
1 C **2** A **3** C **4** C **5** C

TASK 2
6 photo **7** pens **8** Mark **9** weather **10** five o'clock

Reading

TASK 1
11 Do **12** about **13** how **14** their **15** to **16** are

TASK 2
17 Pippa **18** Jak **19** Emmy **20** Jak

SKILLS TEST B

Dictation

My friend has got an old mobile phone and it hasn't got any apps. The screen isn't big, but my friend can go online, send messages and stream music and films.

Listening

TASK 1
1 B **2** B **3** A **4** A **5** A

TASK 2
6 art **7** dictionary **8** Anna **9** train **10** 6 / six o'clock

Reading

TASK 1
11 are **12** them **13** to **14** They **15** the **16** your

TASK 2
17 Lulu **18** Gemma **19** Carl **20** Lulu

UNIT 3

LANGUAGE TEST A

Vocabulary

TASK 1
1 biology **2** sport **3** physics **4** history **5** chemistry
For revision, go to Student's Book: p36

TASK 2
6 art **7** pupil **8** board **9** geography **10** gym
11 timetable **12** bookshelf
For revision, go to Student's Book: p36, p39

TASK 3
13 wore **14** got **15** learned **16** wrote
For revision, go to Student's Book: p39

TASK 4
17 C **18** B **19** B **20** A **21** C
For revision, go to Student's Book: p36, 39

Grammar

TASK 1
22 bought **23** ate **24** knew **25** read **26** won
For revision, go to Student's Book: p38

TASK 2
27 met **28** made **29** were **30** saw **31** walked
For revision, go to Student's Book: p38

TASK 3
32 Amanda and I didn't take the train to school this morning.
33 My mum didn't hear the news this morning.
34 Our teacher didn't speak to us in English today.
35 I didn't do my homework today.
36 We didn't have a long lunch break yesterday.
For revision, go to Student's Book: p38

TASK 4
37 Did you find your homework **38** where did Tom go
39 How long did you stay **40** Did Mark message you
41 No, they weren't
For revision, go to Student's Book: p40

LANGUAGE TEST B

Vocabulary

TASK 1
1 geography **2** maths **3** art **4** sport **5** biology
For revision, go to Student's Book: p36

TASK 2
6 chemistry **7** note **8** office **9** History **10** desks
11 marks **12** ruler
For revision, go to Student's Book: p36, p39

TASK 3
13 got **14** get **15** had **16** wrote
For revision, go to Student's Book: p39

TASK 4
17 C **18** C **19** B **20** B **21** A
For revision, go to Student's Book: p36, p39

TEST ANSWER KEYS

Grammar
TASK 1
22 came **23** went **24** had **25** met **26** saw
For revision, go to Student's Book: p38

TASK 2
27 got **28** found **29** heard **30** spoke **31** spent
For revision, go to Student's Book: p38

TASK 3
32 I didn't wear a uniform at my last school.
33 We didn't see that film at the cinema last month.
34 My brother wasn't in the school office this morning.
35 The teacher didn't give us a lot of homework today.
36 The dictionaries weren't on the bookshelf.
For revision, go to Student's Book: p38

TASK 4
37 Where did you do **38** I didn't **39** Did Molly win
40 Where were you **41** What mark did Sam get
For revision, go to Student's Book: p40

SKILLS TEST A
Dictation
Pupils at many schools often wear uniforms. Some schools have rules about the clothes. Sometimes they just want everyone to dress in the same colours.

Listening
TASK 1
1 C **2** B **3** A **4** C **5** A

TASK 2
6 Her mum went to school in a city and her dad to a village school in France.
7 Her mum went Mondays to Fridays and Saturday mornings, but her dad only went to school on Mondays, Tuesdays, Thursdays and Fridays.
8 They sat at lines of desks, always in the same places.
9 They had homework for every subject at the weekends.
10 Because they went to school in different countries, America and Japan.

Reading
TASK 1
11 B **12** C **13** A **14** A **15** B

TASK 2
16 Because they had to study for exams.
17 Their teachers.
18 Because the pupils weren't tired and could study.
19 For two months.
20 Happy because pupils stay awake in their classes.

SKILLS TEST B
Dictation
Pupils at many schools often wear uniforms. Some schools have rules about the clothes. Sometimes they just want everyone to dress in the same colours.

Listening
TASK 1
1 A **2** C **3** B **4** B **5** B

TASK 2
6 Her mum went to school in a city and her dad went to a village school in France.
7 Her mum went Mondays to Fridays and Saturday mornings, but her dad only went to school on Mondays, Tuesdays, Thursdays and Fridays.
8 They sat at lines of desks, always in the same places.
9 They had homework for every subject at the weekends.
10 Because they went to school in different countries, America and Japan.

Reading
TASK 1
11 C **12** B **13** A **14** B **15** C

TASK 2
16 The students were tired in the mornings.
17 The school decided to start at 9.00 and have lessons on Saturday mornings.
18 The pupils didn't like it because they couldn't do other things on Saturdays.
19 The school decided to start late and finish late.
20 He's happy now.

UNIT 4
LANGUAGE TEST A
Vocabulary
TASK 1
1 pounds **2** dollars **3** euro **4** pence **5** cents
For revision, go to Student's Book: p51

TASK 2
6 sale **7** closed **8** spend **9** receipt **10** cash **11** try
12 bargain **13** cost **14** save **15** sell
For revision, go to Student's Book: p51

TEST ANSWER KEYS

TASK 3
16 library **17** market **18** theatre
19 department store **20** tourist information
For revision, go to Student's Book: p53

TASK 4
21 B **22** C **23** C **24** A **25** B
For revision, go to Student's Book: p48, p53

Grammar

TASK 1
26 prettier **27** newer **28** better **29** higher
30 more difficult **31** thinner **32** further/farther
33 happier **34** more important **35** smaller
For revision, go to Student's Book: p50

TASK 2
36 more exciting **37** busier **38** worse **39** sunnier
40 nearer
For revision, go to Student's Book: p50

TASK 3
41 the best **42** easier **43** the most difficult
44 the happiest **45** the most expensive
For revision, go to Student's Book: p50, p52

TASK 4
46 more **47** the most **48** than **49** is **50** the
For revision, go to Student's Book: p50, p52

LANGUAGE TEST B

Vocabulary

TASK 1
1 supermarket **2** theatre **3** tourist **4** market
5 department
For revision, go to Student's Book: p53

TASK 2
6 pay **7** tried **8** open **9** receipt **10** spent **11** sale
12 save **13** card **14** price **15** bargain
For revision, go to Student's Book: p51

TASK 3
16 library **17** park **18** museum **19** pool **20** theatre
For revision, go to Student's Book: p53

TASK 4
21 C **22** B **23** B **24** A **25** B
For revision, go to Student's Book: p48, p53

Grammar

TASK 1
26 sadder **27** more interesting **28** worse **29** nearer
30 sunnier **31** lower **32** more exciting **33** busier
34 older **35** fatter
For revision, go to Student's Book: p50

TASK 2
36 more important **37** higher **38** further/farther
39 more difficult **40** happier
For revision, go to Student's Book: p50

TASK 3
41 the worst **42** cheaper **43** the funniest
44 the most interesting **45** better
For revision, go to Student's Book: p50, p52

TASK 4
46 than **47** more **48** The **49** the most **50** more
For revision, go to Student's Book: p50, p52

SKILLS TEST A

Dictation
When our parents were young everyone paid with cash. Today we usually pay by card. It's easier than it was to spend more money on things.

Listening

TASK 1
1 B **2** C **3** B **4** C **5** A

TASK 2
6 sandwiches **7** password **8** music shop **9** 50 / fifty
10 7.30 / seven-thirty

Reading

TASK 1
11 but **12** last **13** at **14** it **15** for **16** to

TASK 2
17 F **18** T **19** T **20** F

SKILLS TEST B

Dictation
When our parents were young everyone paid with cash. Today we usually pay by card. It's easier than it was to spend more money on things.

Listening

TASK 1
1 A 2 C 3 B 4 B 5 C

TASK 2
6 gardens 7 24 / twenty-four 8 headphones 9 card 10 10 / ten

Reading

TASK 1
11 some 12 ago 13 in 14 The 15 it 16 to

TASK 2
17 T 18 F 19 T 20 F

UNIT 5

LANGUAGE TEST A

Vocabulary

TASK 1
1 electricity 2 sign 3 classical 4 Sci-fi 5 festival 6 talent 7 guitarist 8 magician 9 theatre 10 comedy

For revision, go to Student's Book: p60, 63

TASK 2
11 romantic 12 exhibition 13 documentary 14 instrument 15 open-air 16 seat 17 artist 18 act 19 action 20 actors

For revision, go to Student's Book: p60, 63

TASK 3
21 B 22 A 23 C 24 B 25 C

For revision, go to Student's Book: p63

Grammar

TASK 1
26 were you watching 27 was listening 28 were working 29 was shining 30 were visiting 31 were studying 32 were practising 33 were you waiting

For revision, go to Student's Book: p62

TASK 2
34 I wasn't playing the guitar all evening.
35 We weren't watching a horror film.
36 You weren't singing very well.
37 The girls weren't doing a magic trick.
38 The girl wasn't going to a talent show.

For revision, go to Student's Book: p62

TASK 3
39 I was watching a movie when you texted me.
40 The children were playing football when the rain started.
41 She was sleeping when the thief came in.
42 Was Jack doing his homework when his friends arrived?
43 We saw some great T-shirts when we were walking in town yesterday.
44 The children weren't playing football when the rain started

For revision, go to Student's Book: p62

LANGUAGE TEST B

Vocabulary

TASK 1
1 classical 2 actor 3 talent 4 music 5 sci-fi 6 perform 7 sign 8 musician 9 comedy 10 theatre

For revision, go to Student's Book: p60, 63

TASK 2
11 horror 12 exhibition 13 concert 14 instrument 15 festival 16 seat 17 artist 18 show 19 Action 20 actor

For revision, go to Student's Book: p60, 63

TASK 3
21 A 22 C 23 A 24 B 25 C

For revision, go to Student's Book: p60, 63

Grammar

TASK 1
26 were you doing 27 was watching 28 were talking 29 was writing 30 were sitting 31 was raining 32 was your brother going 33 was working

For revision, go to Student's Book: p62

TASK 2
34 I wasn't dancing all evening.
35 We weren't listening to classical music.
36 You weren't laughing at the comedian's stories.
37 The boys weren't playing the piano very well.
38 The magician wasn't doing a very difficult trick.

For revision, go to Student's Book: p62

TEST ANSWER KEYS

GOLD experience 2ND EDITION A2

TASK 3
39 We were waiting in the café when our friend came in.
40 I saw a famous singer when I was buying a new pair of shoes yesterday.
41 Grandma fell asleep when we were watching the news last night.
42 I wasn't sleeping when you phoned me.
43 My sisters were playing in the garden when you called.
44 Were you listening to the radio when you heard the news?

For revision, go to Student's Book: p62

SKILLS TEST A

Dictation
Last night I was watching a horror film when I suddenly heard a loud noise. I felt scared but it was only my brother. He wanted to make me jump.

Listening
TASK 1
1 B 2 C 3 B 4 C 5 B

TASK 2
6 7.75 7 bus stop 8 Saturday 9 sister 10 mum

Reading
TASK 1
11 B 12 A 13 C 14 A 15 B 16 C 17 B

TASK 2
18 Because they were unusual for a cinema. They were the kind of seats you see at the beach or on a ship.
19 Because where they will show the film is a secret when you buy the ticket. They only tell you the venue afterwards.
20 She didn't like the length of the film.

SKILLS TEST B

Dictation
Last night I was watching a horror film when I suddenly heard a loud noise. I felt scared but it was only my brother. He wanted to make me jump.

Listening
TASK 1
1 C 2 A 3 C 4 A 5 A

TASK 2
6 4.50 7 concert 8 T-shirt 9 park 10 10 / ten

Reading
TASK 1
11 A 12 B 13 C 14 B 15 A 16 C 17 B

TASK 2
18 Because the money it makes goes to a social project in Cambodia. It does not go to the owner of the business.
19 No, because they were sitting in the open air. She says she loved it and people don't usually like sitting in the rain.
20 No, because people had to dress like characters from the film.

UNIT 6
LANGUAGE TEST A

Vocabulary
TASK 1
1 train 2 plane 3 ferry 4 underground 5 motorbike
6 bike 7 ship 8 helicopter 9 tram 10 coach

For revision, go to Student's Book: p75

TASK 2
11 catch 12 flight 13 foot 14 trip 15 journey
16 ticket 17 travel 18 sail 19 passenger 20 drive

For revision, go to Student's Book: p74, p79

TASK 3
21 by 22 around 23 on 24 for 25 to

For revision, go to Student's Book: p75, p78

Grammar
TASK 1
26 P 27 I 28 I 29 P 30 P 31 I

For revision, go to Student's Book: p74

TASK 2
32 My brother's going to travel to India soon.
33 I'm sure you'll love the food in Japan.
34 Our neighbours aren't going to be at home this weekend.
35 Maria and her mother will probably not / probably won't spend very long here.
36 Is Dad going to buy our train tickets online?
37 Will your visitors arrive on time?

For revision, go to Student's Book: p74

TASK 3
38 am flying 39 is meeting 40 aren't coming
41 is your brother doing 42 are you having
43 is Tom leaving 44 are the children watching

For revision, go to Student's Book: p76

TEST ANSWER KEYS

LANGUAGE TEST B
Vocabulary
TASK 1
1 plane **2** motorbike **3** coach **4** underground **5** ferry **6** bike **7** ship **8** tram **9** helicopter **10** train
For revision, go to Student's Book: p75

TASK 2
11 flight **12** sail **13** foot **14** journey **15** trip **16** drive **17** catch **18** passenger **19** travel **20** ticket
For revision, go to Student's Book: p74, p79

TASK 3
21 on **22** for **23** around **24** to **25** by
For revision, go to Student's Book: p75, p78

Grammar
TASK 1
26 I **27** I **28** P **29** P **30** I **31** P
For revision, go to Student's Book: p74

TASK 2
32 I think Jack will become a successful businessman.
33 I'm sure you'll enjoy your trip to New York.
34 We're going to fly to Spain on Saturday.
35 The children will not / won't want to go to the city tomorrow.
36 What are you going to do at the weekend?
37 I'm not going to spend my holiday in France this year.
For revision, go to Student's Book: p74

TASK 3
38 am studying **39** is playing **40** aren't visiting **41** are you doing **42** is Hannah meeting **43** are your grandparents flying **44** is your mother catching
For revision, go to Student's Book: p76

SKILLS TEST A
Dictation
Next summer my family is going to travel around England. We all enjoy walking so we're going to do lots of that. It'll be fun.

Listening
TASK 1
1 H **2** A **3** E **4** C **5** B

TASK 2
6 island **7** uncle **8** 20 / twenty **9** underground **10** grandmother

Reading
TASK 1
11 A **12** C **13** B **14** C

TASK 2
15 It's crowded and slow.
16 He likes flying, but he doesn't like waiting at the airport.
17 His best friend's family is going to be there, too.
18 He writes a blog, he uses a maps app, and he plays games on it.

SKILLS TEST B
Dictation
Next summer my family is going to travel around England. We all enjoy walking so we're going to do lots of that. It'll be fun.

Listening
TASK 1
1 C **2** E **3** A **4** H **5** F

TASK 2
6 excited **7** train **8** New York **9** beach **10** museums

Reading
TASK 1
11 B **12** A **13** A **14** C

TASK 2
15 She wants to have the opportunity to travel in her work, and to write or guide people.
16 She saw her house with her grandfather sitting in the garden.
17 It doesn't get dark, even in the middle of the night.
18 She texts, she takes photos and she listens to music.

UNIT 7
LANGUAGE TEST A
Vocabulary
TASK 1
1 cycling **2** hockey **3** surfing **4** judo **5** badminton **6** diving **7** skiing **8** coach **9** referee **10** helmet
For revision, go to Student's Book: p84, p87

TASK 2
11 go **12** doing **13** play **14** does **15** go **16** play **17** go **18** went
For revision, go to Student's Book: p87

TASK 3
19 A **20** C **21** A **22** A **23** C **24** C **25** B
For revision, go to Student's Book: p87

TEST ANSWER KEYS

GOLD experience 2ND EDITION A2

Grammar

TASK 1
26 have to   **27** can   **28** can   **29** has to   **30** can
31 have to

For revision, go to Student's Book: p86, p88

TASK 2
32 couldn't   **33** can   **34** can't   **35** Could   **36** couldn't
37 can't   **38** could   **39** can   **40** Could

For revision, go to Student's Book: p86

TASK 3
41 have to   **42** have to   **43** doesn't have to
44 has to   **45** had to   **46** had to   **47** don't have to
48 doesn't have to   **49** didn't have to   **50** has

For revision, go to Student's Book: p88

LANGUAGE TEST B

Vocabulary

TASK 1
1 running   **2** tennis   **3** diving   **4** equipment   **5** cycling
6 helmet   **7** coach   **8** skiing   **9** hockey   **10** referee

For revision, go to Student's Book: p84, p87

TASK 2
11 doing   **12** go   **13** do   **14** play   **15** go   **16** play
17 went   **18** go

For revision, go to Student's Book: p87

TASK 3
19 C   **20** A   **21** A   **22** B   **23** A   **24** A   **25** C

For revision, go to Student's Book: p87

Grammar

TASK 1
26 can   **27** has to   **28** can   **29** have to   **30** can
31 have to

For revision, go to Student's Book: p86, p88

TASK 2
32 Can   **33** couldn't   **34** could   **35** can't   **36** can
37 can't   **38** Could   **39** couldn't   **40** Could

For revision, go to Student's Book: p86

TASK 3
41 don't have to   **42** had to   **43** have to   **44** have to
45 didn't have to   **46** had to   **47** have to
48 doesn't have to   **49** have to   **50** don't have to

For revision, go to Student's Book: p88

SKILLS TEST A

Dictation

I play in my school football team. I need to practise a lot because I can't run very quickly. I also enjoy going swimming and doing judo.

Listening

TASK 1
1 C   **2** A   **3** A   **4** C   **5** C

TASK 2
6 10 / ten   **7** cycling   **8** a surfboard   **9** half past seven
10 skiing

Reading

TASK 1
11 C   **12** B   **13** C   **14** A   **15** A   **16** B   **17** C   **18** B

TASK 2
19 Sports like mountain climbing, mountain biking and skiing; skills like refereeing and coaching.
20 They can get work in sports clubs; they can earn money in their free time.

SKILLS TEST B

Dictation

I play in my school football team. I need to practise a lot because I can't run very quickly. I also enjoy going swimming and doing judo.

Listening

TASK 1
1 A   **2** B   **3** C   **4** B   **5** A

TASK 2
6 18 / eighteen   **7** tennis   **8** goggles   **9** eight o'clock
10 running

Reading

TASK 1
11 B   **12** A   **13** B   **14** C   **15** B   **16** C   **17** B   **18** A

TASK 2
19 They can learn diving, water-skiing; refereeing, sports journalism.
20 They can get a career in sport; they can earn money in their free time.

ТEST ANSWER KEYS

UNIT 8
LANGUAGE TEST A
Vocabulary
TASK 1
1 ocean **2** river **3** desert **4** island **5** lake
For revision, go to Student's Book: p99

TASK 2
6 rain **7** sun **8** storm **9** cloud **10** fog **11** snow **12** wind **13** ice
For revision, go to Student's Book: p99

TASK 3
14 hot **15** cold **16** warm **17** cool **18** hot
For revision, go to Student's Book: p99

TASK 4
19 rains **20** fog **21** ice **22** wet **23** cloudy **24** dry **25** wind
For revision, go to Student's Book: p99

Grammar
TASK 1
26 have **27** have **28** Has **29** have **30** has **31** have
For revision, go to Student's Book: p98

TASK 2
32 ridden **33** learnt / learned **34** put **35** made **36** had **37** bought **38** written **39** read **40** eaten **41** stopped
For revision, go to Student's Book: p98

TASK 3
42 has had **43** has been **44** have visited **45** has ever seen **46** have made **47** have often come **48** have told **49** has written **50** haven't read
For revision, go to Student's Book: p98, p100

LANGUAGE TEST B
Vocabulary
TASK 1
1 hill **2** rainforest **3** coast **4** desert **5** ocean
For revision, go to Student's Book: p99

TASK 2
6 rain **7** sun **8** storm **9** cloud **10** fog **11** snow **12** wind **13** ice
For revision, go to Student's Book: p99

TASK 3
14 boiling **15** cold **16** warm **17** dry **18** freezing
For revision, go to Student's Book: p99

TASK 4
19 snows **20** fog **21** sun **22** snowy **23** dry **24** sunny **25** ice
For revision, go to Student's Book: p99

Grammar
TASK 1
26 have **27** have **28** has **29** have **30** have **31** Has
For revision, go to Student's Book: p98

TASK 2
32 flown **33** bought **34** swum **35** taken **36** written **37** worn **38** eaten **39** seen **40** heard **41** done
For revision, go to Student's Book: p98

TASK 3
42 have always wanted **43** has been **44** has told **45** have seen **46** have also read **47** have started **48** haven't learnt/learned **49** have had **50** has ever visited
For revision, go to Student's Book: p98, p100

SKILLS TEST A
Dictation
Last August I went camping with a friend. We spent three days at a campsite on an island. We really enjoyed sleeping in a tent.

Listening
TASK 1
1 C **2** B **3** B **4** C **5** A

TASK 2
6 looking out of the window **7** It was raining. **8** the monkeys **9** They climbed a mountain. **10** surfing

Reading
TASK 1
11 B **12** C **13** A **14** B **15** A **16** C **17** B

TASK 2
18 the fourth Sunday in September
19 long river
20 by the sea, not far from some mountains

SKILLS TEST B

Dictation
Last August I went camping with a friend. We spent three days at a campsite on an island. We really enjoyed sleeping in a tent.

Listening
TASK 1
1 A **2** A **3** C **4** A **5** B

TASK 2
6 watching films **7** warm **8** the elephants
9 They went swimming in a lake. **10** canoeing

Reading
TASK 1
11 B **12** C **13** B **14** A **15** C **16** B **17** A

TASK 2
18 11 December
19 to train for the Tour de France
20 She enjoyed the sunshine and took photos.

UNIT 9
LANGUAGE TEST A

Vocabulary
TASK 1
1 chips **2** omelette **3** sandwich **4** soup **5** cake
6 salad **7** pasta **8** steak **9** cereal
For revision, go to Student's Book: p111

TASK 2
10 have **11** fresh **12** go for **13** air **14** get **15** find
For revision, go to Student's Book: p111

TASK 3
16 toothache **17** bakes **18** sick **19** snacks
20 healthy **21** barbecue **22** temperature
23 vegetables **24** boil **25** biscuit
For revision, go to Student's Book: p111, p114

Grammar
TASK 1
26 will win **27** get **28** won't go **29** give
30 will you come **31** are **32** will feel **33** don't leave
34 will have / 'll have **35** cooks
For revision, go to Student's Book: p110

TASK 2
36 If Lisa has a cold, I'll look after the children.
37 You will need your umbrella if you go out today.
38 What will the teacher say if the children don't do their homework?
39 If I make a cheese sandwich, will you have one too?
40 The new restaurant will open next Monday if everything is ready.
For revision, go to Student's Book: p110

TASK 3
41 should **42** shouldn't **43** should **44** shouldn't
45 should
For revision, go to Student's Book: p112

LANGUAGE TEST B

Vocabulary
TASK 1
1 steak **2** salad **3** pasta **4** sandwich **5** cereal
6 chips **7** cake **8** soup **9** omelette
For revision, go to Student's Book: p111

TASK 2
10 had **11** fresh **12** fried **13** went for **14** get
15 get
For revision, go to Student's Book: p111

TASK 3
16 time **17** grill **18** bake **19** snack **20** stomach
21 boiled **22** burger **23** barbecue **24** sick
25 temperature
For revision, go to Student's Book: p111, p114

Grammar
TASK 1
26 will feel / 'll feel **27** are / 're **28** won't go **29** has
30 will you make **31** don't want **32** will help
33 doesn't leave **34** will have / 'll have **35** don't wear
For revision, go to Student's Book: p110

TASK 2
36 I'll buy/will buy the cinema tickets if they aren't/are not too expensive.
37 If it's a nice day on Saturday, we'll go to the beach.
38 What will Mike say if the girls get home late?
39 If the students do well in their test, the teacher will show them a film.
40 If Mary goes for a walk this evening, will you go with her?
For revision, go to Student's Book: p110

TASK 3
41 should **42** shouldn't **43** should **44** shouldn't
45 should
For revision, go to Student's Book: p112

SKILLS TEST A

Dictation

If we go to a restaurant for dinner this evening, I'll have steak, chips and salad. I always choose that because it's my favourite meal.

Listening

TASK 1
1 Tuesday 2 4.45 3 butter 4 225 5 cakes

TASK 2
6 Thursday 7 4 / four 8 eggs 9 175 10 biscuits

Reading

TASK 1
11 C 12 B 13 A 14 B

TASK 2
15 around ten years ago
16 We can see similar types of show in different countries around the world.
17 It's exciting to know who will leave the show next. Also, interesting accidents sometimes happen.
18 It can encourage people to bake at home.

SKILLS TEST B

Dictation

If we go to a restaurant for dinner this evening, I'll have steak, chips and salad. I always choose that because it's my favourite meal.

Listening

TASK 1
1 Thursday 2 4.15 3 eggs 4 175 5 biscuits

TASK 2
6 Tuesday 7 5 / five 8 butter 9 225 10 cakes

Reading

TASK 1
11 B 12 C 13 C 14 A

TASK 2
15 In 1990.
16 We can see similar types of show in many countries around the world.
17 People who want to take part in the show, who are up to the age of sixteen.
18 People enjoy learning about different types of food, and how to cook it.

REVIEW (UNITS 1–3)

LANGUAGE TEST A

Vocabulary

TASK 1
1 headphones 2 mouse 3 bookshelf 4 geography 5 camping 6 baking 7 sleepover

TASK 2
8 wear 9 do 10 play 11 get 12 collect 13 message 14 go 15 chat

TASK 3
16 B 17 C 18 B 19 A 20 C 21 C 22 A 23 C 24 B 25 C

Grammar

TASK 1
26 How often does she go shopping?
27 When did you visit your gran?
28 I usually do my homework in the evening.
29 Is your dad working in London now?
30 We don't have maths on Fridays.

TASK 2
31 Do you enjoy 32 doesn't like, loves 33 didn't learn, was at primary school 34 Are you doing 35 did you go 36 'm not watching, 'm reading

TASK 3
37 some 38 was 39 front 40 is 41 Did

LANGUAGE TEST B

Vocabulary

TASK 1
1 keyboard 2 timetable 3 singing 4 uniform 5 screen 6 biology 7 comics

TASK 2
8 get 9 Click 10 have 11 wear 12 play 13 get 14 collect 15 go

TASK 3
16 C 17 C 18 B 19 B 20 A 21 A 22 C 23 A 24 A 25 B

Grammar

TASK 1
26 We don't often go shopping after school.
27 My laptop isn't working at the moment.
28 Did the teacher give us any homework for this evening?
29 Do you enjoy chatting online?
30 My brother doesn't like cheese sandwiches.

TEST ANSWER KEYS

TASK 2
31 didn't have, had **32** usually go, walked.
33 Is your dad driving **34** loves **35** Did you send, were
36 don't enjoy, learning

TASK 3
37 last **38** did **39** am **40** is **41** Do

WRITING
Sample answer

Hi Mark,
Last weekend I stayed with my friend, Sally. She lives near London.
Her brother loves playing football. On Saturday he was in a competition and we watched the game. His team won! He was very happy. On Sunday we played computer games and watched some films on television.
How about you? Did you have a good weekend?
Love,
Karen

SPEAKING
Sample Answer
Student A

TASK 1
I'm six. I live in a small house about ten killometres from the city. It's small, but it has a large garden, and I really like it.

TASK 2
I spend about three or four hours a week online. I don't go online every evening. I usually go online at the weekend. I like chatting online with friends. I also like watching TV online. I don't watch many films online, because I prefer watching films at the cinema. I go to the cinema once a month. My favourite website is a music site. I like listening to new music, and I visit it about once a week. All my friends like it, and we like chatting about the things we listen to.

Student B

TASK 1
I'm fifteen. I live in an apartment near the centre of town. I live there with my parents and my two brothers.

TASK 2
I live far from my school, so I usually go by bus. My Dad sometimes drives me to school, but I never walk. I have a lot of homework, and I usually do it at home, in my room. I sometimes do it at my grandmother's house, because we go there at the weekend. My favourite day at school is Thursday. We have English lessons in the afternoon. That's my favourite subject. I like it because it's quite easy for me. Some of my friends like studying English, but some don't. They don't like it because it's difficult for them.

REVIEW (UNITS 4–6)
LANGUAGE TEST A
Vocabulary
TASK 1
1 fishing **2** screen **3** notebook **4** journey **5** magician
6 fiction **7** platform **8** bargain

TASK 2
9 catch **10** ride **11** wear **12** pay **13** perform
14 travel **15** get

TASK 3
16 C **17** A **18** B **19** A **20** C **21** A **22** A
23 A **24** B

Grammar
TASK 1
25 Do you walk **26** I'm always **27** was having
28 am meeting **29** the busiest

TASK 2
30 go, 're travelling **31** arranged, 'm playing
32 more expensive, the most expensive
33 was waiting, started **34** went, didn't buy

TASK 3
35 are **36** ago **37** were **38** any **39** many **40** the
41 went **42** than **43** to **44** will

LANGUAGE TEST B
Vocabulary
TASK 1
1 romantic **2** helicopter **3** guitarists **4** scary **5** price
6 comedian **7** pupils **8** library

TASK 2
9 perform **10** drive **11** saved **12** go **13** made
14 take **15** visit

TASK 3
16 C **17** B **18** C **19** C **20** B **21** C **22** B **23** B
24 A **25** C

TEST ANSWER KEYS

GOLD experience 2ND EDITION **A2**

Grammar

TASK 1
26 usually cooks **27** easier **28** finished
29 are you waiting **30** is playing

TASK 2
31 cheaper, cheapest **32** loves, doesn't enjoy
33 did, 'm going to relax **34** works, 's working
35 was cooking, heard

TASK 3
36 ago **37** many **38** than **39** any **40** the
41 to **42** were **43** are **44** last **45** Will

WRITING

Sample answer
Alice did her maths homework at home.
When she was walking to school the next day, she remembered that she didn't have her homework with her. It was at home!
Her mum came to the school and gave Alice the homework.

SPEAKING

Sample Answer
Student A

TASK 1
A: I like playing video games. I think they're fun.
B: Yes, me too. I like them because I can sometimes learn things, too.
A: I always love listening to music.
B: I really enjoy downloading songs onto my phone and listening to them with headphones.
A: In my opinion, painting is boring. That's why I don't like it.
B: I like it, because I'm good at painting.
A: I don't really enjoy sports.
B: I do. But I prefer going to the cinema.
A: Me too. I like action films.
B: And I enjoy books, too. I like spending time in my room, reading.

TASK 2
Do you prefer to go on holiday to a different country or stay in your own country? (Why?)
I prefer going to a different country because I can see and do different things. I also enjoy trying new food from different places. It's more interesting than eating things that I always eat.
Which place would you like to go to on holiday in the future? (Why?)
I'd like to go to the mountains. I often go to the beach on holiday, so it would be nice to try something different. I like walking, so going to the mountains would be a good chance to be outdoors and get some exercise.

Student B

TASK 1
A: I like playing video games. I think they're fun.
B: Yes, me too. I like them because I can sometimes learn things, too.
A: I always love listening to music.
B: I really enjoy downloading songs onto my phone and listening to them with headphones.
A: In my opinion, painting is boring. That's why I don't like it.
B: I like it, because I'm good at painting.
A: I don't really enjoy sports.
B: I do. But I prefer going to the cinema.
A: Me too. I like action films.
B: And I enjoy books, too. I like spending time in my room, reading.

TASK 2
Do you prefer to go on holiday to a different country or stay in your own country? (Why?)
I prefer going to a different country because I can see and do different things. I also enjoy trying new food from different places. It's more interesting than eating things that I always eat.
Which place would you like to go to on holiday in the future? (Why?)
I'd like to go to the mountains. I often go to the beach on holiday, so it would be nice to try something different. I like walking, so going to the mountains would be a good chance to be outdoors and get some exercise.

REVIEW (UNITS 7–9)

LANGUAGE TEST A

Vocabulary

TASK 1
1 island **2** zero **3** bee **4** knife **5** sick **6** healthy
7 equipment **8** practice

TASK 2
9 have **10** for **11** instructions **12** dry **13** doing
14 helmet **15** racket

TASK 3
16 B **17** A **18** C **19** C **20** A **21** C **22** B **23** B
24 C **25** B

Grammar

TASK 1
26 couldn't **27** never **28** can't **29** will feel **30** is

TASK 2
31 see, will buy/am going to buy **32** Have you ever slept
33 will have, go **34** has never been **35** Have you eaten

TASK 3
36 be **37** ago **38** if **39** went **40** can **41** better
42 will **43** am

Photocopiable © Pearson Education Limited 2018

LANGUAGE TEST B
Vocabulary
TASK 1
1 sick **2** spoon **3** practice **4** islands **5** healthy **6** referee **7** lake **8** equipment

TASK 2
9 racket **10** grilling **11** helmet **12** have **13** boiling **14** find **15** going

TASK 3
16 C **17** C **18** B **19** A **20** B **21** C **22** A **23** B **24** C **25** A

Grammar
TASK 1
26 is **27** don't have to **28** could **29** will **30** ever

TASK 2
31 Have you ever eaten **32** gives, will get **33** has never been **34** will drive, come **35** haven't drunk

TASK 3
36 last **37** couldn't **38** better **39** will **40** if **41** won't **42** are **43** don't/never

WRITING
Sample answer

Max was worried when he was baking a cake for his school cooking competition. He was very pleased when he won first prize – best teen cook!

He shared the cake with his friends. They thought that it was delicious. Max really was a good cook!

SPEAKING
Sample Answer
Student A
TASK 1
A: I don't really like going to the theatre. I think it can be boring.
B: Yes, and plays can last a long time.
A: I like going to restaurants.
B: Me too, but I don't go very often. They're expensive
A: I like concerts and festivals, because I can go with my friends and have a good time.
B: In my opinion, concerts aren't so good. It's better to listen to music at home, because you can hear more clearly.
A: I love the cinema.
B: I don't. It's annoying when someone behind you talks, or makes a noise.
A: I don't go to museums very often.
B: Nor do I, but I like them. You can learn interesting things.

TASK 2
Do you prefer doing the same thing every weekend or doing different things? (Why?)
Of course, I like to do different things every weekend, because it's boring to do the same thing all the time. Also, I don't go out every weekend, because it can be expensive.

Do you prefer being at home, or doing sport? (Why?)
If the weather is nice, then I like going out and doing something in the fresh air. I like running and playing football. If the weather is bad, then I stay at home. It's nice to be inside with a book or to watch something on TV when it's cold or wet outside.

Student B
TASK 1
A: I don't really like going to the theatre. I think it can be boring.
B: Yes, and plays can last a long time.
A: I like going to restaurants.
B: Me too, but I don't go very often. They're expensive
A: I like concerts and festivals, because I can go with my friends and have a good time.
B: In my opinion, concerts aren't so good. It's better to listen to music at home, because you can hear more clearly.
A: I love the cinema.
B: I don't. It's annoying when someone behind you talks, or makes a noise.
A: I don't go to museums very often.
B: Nor do I, but I like them. You can learn interesting things.

TASK 2
Do you prefer doing the same thing every weekend or doing different things? (Why?)
Of course, I like to do different things every weekend, because it's boring to do the same thing all the time. Also, I don't go out every weekend, because it can be expensive.

Do you prefer being at home, or doing sport? (Why?)
If the weather is nice, then I like going out and doing something in the fresh air. I like running and playing football. If the weather is bad, then I stay at home. It's nice to be inside with a book or to watch something on TV when it's cold or wet outside.

TEST ANSWER KEYS

END OF YEAR
LANGUAGE TEST A

Listening
TASK 1
1 A **2** C **3** B **4** A **5** B
TASK 2
6 Black **7** Transport **8** bus **9** 9.15 **10** quiz

Language
TASK 1
11 C **12** A **13** B **14** A **15** C **16** B **17** B **18** C
TASK 2
19 are **20** was **21** ago **22** were **23** to **24** than
25 Have

Reading
TASK 1
26 A **27** B **28** A **29** C **30** B
TASK 2
31 B **32** A **33** B **34** C **35** C

LANGUAGE TEST B

Listening
TASK 1
1 B **2** B **3** C **4** B **5** A
TASK 2
6 Farmer **7** Science **8** train **9** 9.50 **10** film

Language
TASK 1
11 B **12** A **13** B **14** C **15** A **16** C **17** B **18** A
TASK 2
19 are **20** haven't **21** Did **22** am **23** last
24 couldn't **25** to

Reading
TASK 1
26 A **27** B **28** C **29** A **30** C
TASK 2
31 C **32** B **33** C **34** B **35** A

WRITING
Sample answer
TASK 1

Hi Alex,
I hope you're well!
Would you like to visit me? We haven't met for a long time. Next weekend is good for me, and there's a festival on in the park near my house. We can go to it together if you like. What do you think?
Write soon,
Karl

Sample answer
TASK 2

Ben and his parents arrived late at the airport. They were very tired after their long journey.
They went by taxi to their hotel. It was a nice place near the sea. They were very happy to arrive, and went straight to bed.
The next day, they were enjoying a great day at the hotel. Ben went swimming in the hotel pool. His father slept, and his mother enjoyed a delicious ice cream!

SPEAKING
Sample answers
Student A
TASK 1

I don't do sport every day, but I do it quite often. I usually do sport twice a week at school with my friends. At other times, I do it alone. The last time I did any sport was yesterday. I played football at school.
My favourite sport is running. I like listening to music with headphones when I run. I often run next to a river near my house.

TASK 2

A: I don't go to museums very often. Do you?
B: No, I don't. But I like them. They sometimes have interesting things. I often go to shopping centres.
A: Me too. I go every weekend with my mum. I don't like them very much.
B: No. In my opinion, they are often crowded.
A: Forests aren't crowded.
B: That's right! They are usually very nice places. I like walking in forests.
A: Have you ever been to the theatre?
B: Yes, of course. I enjoy going, but I don't go often.
A: I go to the swimming pool once a week. I'm learning to swim.
B: I can't swim, so I never go. Can you play football?
A: Yes, but I prefer watching! I watch on TV. I don't go to football stadiums. You enjoy the match more if you watch on TV.
A: Which place do you like best? I think I like the swimming pool best. How about you?
B: For me, the forest. I like nature, and animals, and it's healthy to be in a forest, in my opinion.

TEST ANSWER KEYS

Student B

TASK 1

I usually watch films at home, but I sometimes go to the cinema with my family. I'd like to see the new *Star Wars* film next, because lots of people have told me that it's very good. I don't usually like science-fiction films. I like watching drama and comedy films most.

The best film that I've ever seen was on TV in my house. My brother told me that it was very good, so I watched it. It's about a boy who wants to grow up to become a footballer, so he trains very hard, and one day becomes captain of a football team. It's sometimes sad and sometimes funny, and I've watched it three times!

TASK 2

A: I don't go to museums very often. Do you?

B: No, I don't. But I like them. They sometimes have interesting things. I often go to shopping centres.

A: Me too. I go every weekend with my mum. I don't like them very much.

B: No. In my opinion, they are often crowded.

A: Forests aren't crowded.

B: That's right! They are usually very nice places. I like walking in forests.

A: Have you ever been to the theatre?

B: Yes, of course. I enjoy going, but I don't go often.

A: I go to the swimming pool once a week. I'm learning to swim.

B: I can't swim, so I never go. Can you play football?

A: Yes, but I prefer watching! I watch on TV. I don't go to football stadiums. You enjoy the match more if you watch on TV.

A: Which place do you like best? I think I like the swimming pool best. How about you?

B: For me, the forest. I like nature, and animals, and it's healthy to be in a forest, in my opinion.

WRITING

25 score points in total. Responses are scored according to how well students perform against the following criteria:

Writing score rubric for A2 (5 = B1; 3 = A2; 1 = A1)

	CONTENT	TASK ACHIEVEMENT	ORGANISATION AND STRUCTURE	ACCURACY	RANGE
BAND 5	Includes all three things in the reply. The reader can understand them clearly.	Message includes phrases for describing likes, wants, inviting, suggesting, thanking etc. They are usually correct. The reader can understand the message easily.	Uses simple linking words (e.g. *and, but*) correctly.	Uses simple grammar and vocabulary, usually correctly.	Shows a good range of simple grammatical forms. Can use a range of vocabulary when writing about everyday situations.
BAND 4	Contains some elements of Band 3 and some elements of Band 5.				
BAND 3	Includes at least two things in the reply. The reader can mostly understand them.	The reader rarely tries hard to understand the message.	Uses simple linking words (e.g. *and, but*) correctly.	Uses simple grammar and vocabulary, often correctly.	Has an adequate range of grammatical structures. Often uses a range of vocabulary when talking about everyday situations.
BAND 2	Contains some elements of Band 1 and some elements of Band 3.				
BAND 1	Poor attempt at the task. Most elements of the task are not communicated.	The reader must sometimes try hard to understand the message.	Uses simple linking words (e.g. *and, but*).	Uses simple grammar and vocabulary, with many errors.	Only uses a few grammatical forms. Can use some isolated words and phrases.
BAND 0	No or little writing produced.				

TEST ANSWER KEYS

GOLD experience 2ND EDITION **A2**

SPEAKING

25 score points in total. Responses are scored according to how well students perform against the following criteria:

Speaking score rubric for A2 (5 = B1; 3 = A2; 1 = A1)

	TASK ACHIEVEMENT	RANGE	SPOKEN INTERACTION	SPOKEN PRODUCTION & FLUENCY	ACCURACY
BAND 5	Very good attempt at the task. All elements of the task are communicated.	Shows a good range of simple grammatical forms. Can use a range of vocabulary when talking about everyday situations.	Can keep a conversation going. Doesn't need any extra prompting and support.	Can keep talking without hesitating or repeating words often.	Pronunciation is mostly clear, and can pronounce words and whole phrases well. Grammar is accurate and contains few mistakes.
BAND 4	Contains some elements of Band 3 and some elements of Band 5.				
BAND 3	Satisfactory attempt at the task. Most elements of the task are communicated	Has an adequate range of grammatical structures. Often uses a range of vocabulary when talking about everyday situations.	Can keep a simple conversation going Needs some extra prompting and support.	Can keep talking, although may need to hesitate to think of words, or repeat items.	Pronunciation is mostly clear, but not always easy to understand. Grammar is mostly accurate and contains some mistakes.
BAND 2	Contains some elements of Band 1 and some elements of Band 3.				
BAND 1	Poor attempt at the task. Most elements of the task are not communicated.	Only uses a few grammatical forms. Can use some isolated words and phrases phrases.	Has difficulty keeping any conversation going. Needs a lot of extra prompting and support.	Often hesitates, or repeats the same basic words.	Pronunciation is usually difficult to understand. Grammar contains some mistakes, which makes the message difficult to understand.
BAND 0	Incomprehensible, silent or only speaking first language.				

TESTS AUDIOSCRIPTS

Unit 1 Skills Test Dictation
My friend has many interesting hobbies. She enjoys collecting postcards and sometimes goes fishing with her dad. I think that is awesome.

Unit 1 Skills Test Listening
Hi Mark. It's Annie. I hope you're OK. I'm calling with some exciting news! Do you know about the talent competition? It's at Bank College. It's for their students, and students from our school and Park School too. It's on Saturday, but people have to give their names before Thursday. The competition starts at ten thirty and finishes at four. Students go to room fifteen and give their names to Miss Edwards, that's E–D–W–A–R–D–S, and then the competition is in the hall.

I think you can win! Eva and Maria from our class are in the competition too. They're dancing, but they aren't very good!

So, phone the college and give them your name. Speak to Mr Barnet – that's B–A–R–N–E–T. He's there in the mornings. His number is 02779 381 420. And don't be late! The first prize is £100 and the second is £50. That's a lot of money!

Unit 2 Skills Test Dictation
My friend has got an old mobile phone and it hasn't got any apps. The screen isn't big, but my friend can go online, send messages and stream music and films.

Unit 2 Skills Test Listening
1
A: Jack, why are you here? It's Thursday. You're usually at art club.
B: It's on Monday now. I'm coming to the computer club today.
A: That's cool. The teacher's very good. He does the photo club on Wednesdays too.
B: Really? That's interesting! Oh no. I've got music club then!

2
A: Why are you taking a photograph of the sky, Maria?
B: It's for a competition! Do you like this digital camera? It's my brother's. I want to win the competition.
A: Is there a good prize?
B: The winner gets a new dictionary, but there are pens for the next three people.

3
A: Hello! Where are you?
B: Oh, hi Olly. I'm in the café with Mark.
A: Great. It's Anna's birthday today. Do you and Mark want to go to her party?
B: Brilliant! My brother Jimmy can drive us in his new car!

4
A: Here's my new phone. It's got lots of apps!
B: My favourite one is the weather app – I look at it in the mornings. Then I can wear the right clothes. And I love the sports news app. For all the latest games!
A: Ah – I haven't got those. But ask me 'What time's the next train?' and I can tell you. It's in fifteen minutes!
B: Great! But we aren't going anywhere. Look! It's raining!

5
A: Hello. It's Amy. Are you doing your homework? Help me, please! I don't understand the technology questions.
B: I'm watching a TV programme right now. It's really cool. It finishes at five o'clock. Then mum's cooking dinner for five thirty. I usually finish dinner at six.
A: I have dinner when your TV show finishes. Can you call me after you eat? I'm trying to do this homework, but it's really difficult!
B: No problem. I'll call you then.

Unit 3 Skills Test Dictation
Pupils at many schools often wear uniforms. Some schools have rules about the clothes. Sometimes they just want everyone to dress in the same colours.

Unit 3 Skills Test Listening
A: Where did your dad go to school, Jenna?
B: He went to a small school in a French village. There were only sixty-five pupils. Today, there's a new school there and it's got 200.
A: Wow! And your mum?
B: Oh, she was at a city school. Her first school had 500 pupils.
A: Were their school hours the same as ours?
B: Well, today, we go to school every day, Monday to Friday, but dad never had school on Wednesdays. But poor mum had school on Saturday mornings too!
A: That's terrible! Were their classrooms like ours today?
B: Oh no. They sat in lines of desks, always next to the same person. I prefer our classrooms, sitting around tables in groups.
A: Me too, and it's good to change groups sometimes, too. Did your mum and dad get a lot of homework?
B: When they were teenagers like us they had homework for every subject at the weekend.
A: Oh no! We're lucky. Our class have only got English and maths homework this weekend.
And I did my maths this afternoon in the library, so I only need to do English at home.
B: Tell me about your parents. What were their schools like?
A: Well, Mum is from Japan and Dad is American, so they had very different schools!
B: Oh, really? So, where did *you* first go to school?
A: We moved here when I was two years old, so I went to an English school, like you.

Unit 4 Skills Test Dictation

When our parents were young everyone paid with cash. Today we usually pay by card. It's easier than it was to spend more money on things.

Unit 4 Skills Test Listening

1

A: I went to the new shopping centre by bus today. It was a long way!

B: You're right. I stayed over with Katy last night and we walked there together this morning. It's really close to her house.

A: Do you like the centre?

B: It's smaller than I thought, but the gardens around it are lovely to walk through. We sat there and ate some sandwiches from the café.

2

A: Did you buy anything in that twenty-four hour online sale yesterday?

B: I wanted to get a really cheap jacket that I saw in the shop last week, but I forgot my password.

A: It's easy to get a new password. You click on 'forgot my password' and they send a link.

B: I know and yes, I did! But they didn't send a link. I phoned the shop and there was no answer. So, no jacket!

3

Sarah – hi! It's Jed. I'm buying Dad's birthday present and I'm in the music shop. Dad loves music and I remember Mum bought him some speakers last year. There are some cool headphones here and they're a good price. What do you think? I know he wants some CDs, but I don't know which ones. If you don't agree with the headphones, we can change them at the weekend.

4

A: Hi Annie! I like your sunglasses. Were they expensive?

B: Yes! They were a mistake! I saw them in the department store and I thought they were lovely and very cheap – only fifteen euros. I used my card to pay and I didn't check the screen. Later I found that I paid 150 euros for them!

A: Wow! A few years ago I paid fifty euros for some – I thought that was expensive! But they were very good. For 150 euros your sunglasses are probably extra, extra special!

5

A: I've got a new Saturday job. I'm a shop assistant in the new clothes shop.

B: Cool! Are you enjoying it?

A: Yes, I am. I work from 10.00 until 7.30. It's a bit late, but that's OK. I also get cheaper clothes – and that is very good! The customers are usually nice, but sometimes they're rude and get angry when I make mistakes with their money. But I'm learning and it's fun!

Unit 5 Skills Test Dictation

Last night I was watching a horror film when I suddenly heard a loud noise. I felt scared, but it was only my brother. He wanted to make me jump.

Unit 5 Skills Test Listening

1

A: How much did you pay for your cinema ticket?

B: I can't remember. £3.25, I think. Let me see. It was £4.50 actually.

A: That's good. I paid £7.75 for mine. Tickets cost more now I'm sixteen.

B: Oh, I'll be sixteen next month. I should go to the cinema a lot in the next few weeks!

2

A: Shall we meet at the bus stop at six this evening, Tessa?

B: OK. Then we should get to the city centre by six-thirty.

A: That's good because the concert begins at seven.

B: Excellent! See you at six, then.

3

A: I bought this at the festival on Saturday, Helena. Do you like it?

B: It's a great T-shirt, Nick. And I got a bag there. Look.

A: Oh I like that. Did you buy a hat too? I didn't buy one, but they had some great ones.

B: I wanted to get one too, but I didn't have enough money.

4

A: I'm sorry I didn't go to the cinema with you yesterday, Andy. My sister had some pictures in an art exhibition and I had to go and see them.

B: That's OK, Fatima. It wasn't a very good film actually.

A: There's an open air concert in the park tomorrow. Would you like to go to that?

B: Great idea!

5

A: How did you get on in the talent show, Josh?

B: It was great, aunt Jenny. But it didn't finish until ten o'clock. And the last bus home goes at ten to.

A: So how did you get home?

B: I called mum and she picked me up. She got there by ten past ten, so I wasn't home very late.

Unit 6 Skills Test Dictation

Next summer my family is going to travel around England. We all enjoy walking so we're going to do lots of that. It'll be fun.

Unit 6 Skills Test Listening

A: At school today, Dad, we were talking about how we're all going to go on holiday.

B: OK.

A: Everyone's going to use a different type of transport. Abdul's going to visit a little island. He's going to get there by helicopter. He's very excited!

B: What about your best friend, Bella?

A: She's going to her uncle's. She usually goes by train, but this time they're going to take the coach. It's not so expensive.

B: Right.

A: Carlo's lucky. He's going to visit New York. He's going to fly there.

B: Of course.

A: Then there's Diana. She and her family are going to spend a week at the beach. It's only twenty kilometres away, so they're going to cycle there.

B: Wow! And what about Eddie?

A: Usually his family stays here and goes to different places on the underground. But this time they're going to sail to an island.

B: Great.

A: And there's Flora. She's going to visit her grandmother. She lives in a big city. Flora's going to get there by train. Then, her grandma's going to drive her around the city to visit museums and do lots of shopping.

Unit 7 Skills Test Dictation

I play in my school football team. I need to practise a lot because I can't run very quickly. I also enjoy going swimming and doing judo.

Unit 7 Skills Test Listening

1

A: This basketball shirt isn't yours, is it Paul? The one with number ten on it?

B: No, that's Tom's. I've got eighteen on mine.

A: Oh right. I thought you were fifteen.

B: No, not this year.

2

A: I think I like tennis best now.

B: Do you, Sandro? I thought basketball was your favourite sport.

A: It was, Leila, but I'm not so keen on it now. What about you?

B: It's still cycling for me. And I'm sure it always will be.

3

A: Did you find the surfboard that you wanted at the sports shop, Melissa?

B: No. They didn't have the right style. But I got these great goggles.

A: They're good. Do they sell wetsuits? I need a new one and so do you.

B: Yes, they've got some there.

4

A: Does your hockey practice start at six, Ned? You need to get there on time.

B: It's at eight today. I have to get there for half past seven. We're going to have a team talk and a warm-up before it starts.

A: OK. Well, have a nice time.

5

A: Shall we go skiing in the mountains this weekend, Zara?

B: OK, Charlie. But remember I've only tried it once or twice before.

A: That's OK. I've done it lots and I can help you. And next time, you can help me with my diving at the swimming pool. You're brilliant at that.

B: All right. But I have to go and watch my little brother in a running race later this afternoon.

Unit 8 Skills Test Dictation

Last August I went camping with a friend. We spent three days at a campsite on an island. We really enjoyed sleeping in a tent.

Unit 8 Skills Test Listening

A: That was a great holiday in South Africa, wasn't it, Tom?

B: It was brilliant, Kirsty. I even enjoyed the flight. The best thing was watching some great films.

A: Yes. But I preferred looking out of the window at Africa below us. And the food wasn't bad.

B: I was surprised by the weather when we arrived.

A: I expected it to be warm. And it was raining.

B: At least it wasn't windy.

A: Which animals did you like best when we went on safari? I liked the elephants most.

B: They were amazing. I loved the lions, too. But my favourites were the monkeys.

A: Can you remember what we did on Saturday?

B: Erm, was that the day we climbed a mountain?

A: No, that was Friday. I remember now – we went for a walk in the desert. It was beautiful.

B: I preferred it when we went swimming on Sunday. The water in that lake was so cool.

A: It was great doing all those different sports. I was surprised Mum and Dad came diving with us.

B: Yeah, because Mum stayed on the beach when we went surfing and Dad just watched when we went canoeing. What a great holiday it was!

Unit 9 Skills Test Dictation

If we go to a restaurant for dinner this evening, I'll have steak, chips and salad. I always choose that because it's my favourite meal.

Unit 9 Skills Test Listening

OK I want to tell you about a special cooking lesson you're going to have next week. You'll be in two groups, A and B. If you look at your paper, you'll see which group you are in.

So when is the lesson? For Group A, it's on Tuesday and the other group will have it on Thursday.

And the lessons are at different times. Group B's lesson will be at quarter past four. The other group's will be a bit later, at quarter to five. OK?

Please bring some things from home for the lesson. I'd like the students in Group B to bring eggs and the others to bring butter.

And could you all bring some sugar. Group A will need 225 grams, but the other group will only need 175 grams. The school will give you all the other things that you need.

So what are you going to make? Well, the B group is going to make biscuits and the A group is going to make cakes. I think you'll all have a lot of fun.

End of Year Test Listening Task 1

1

A: Did you enjoy sports camp, Natasha?

B: I loved it. Josh, didn't you? It was so good to get coaching in all those different sports.

A: Yes, it was. Tennis was my favourite.

B: I loved it too. But I think I enjoyed cycling more. The only thing I didn't much like was basketball.

A: Oh, I loved that. I enjoyed everything.

2

A: What a lovely sunny day today!

B: I know. It makes me so happy after all that rain on Saturday and Sunday. It's windy, but I don't mind that.

A: At least it wasn't foggy at the weekend, like it was last Wednesday.

B: That's true.

3

A: Can we make something, please, Dad? I'm hungry.

B: Me too. The quickest thing would be to make a barbecue.

A: It's raining, isn't it? Or we can grill these fish.

B: OK. I'll do that. And you can boil some potatoes.

4

A: Is this your sister in this photo, Nick? She's got lovely long hair. And she's got glasses like yours.

B: No, that's my cousin.

A: Oh.

B: My sister's got glasses too, but her hair is much shorter. She says she's going to grow it next year.

5

A: OK class, have you got everything you need for our trip?

B: I haven't got my dictionary, Miss Brown. I'm sorry.

A: You won't need that today, Fred. Just a camera, a notebook and a pen.

B: Oh, can someone lend me a pen, please? I can use the camera on my phone.

End of Year Test Listening Task 2

OK, class. Listen please.

We're a big class, so we're going to have two different class trips next week – one for boys and one for girls. Both trips are going on Monday.

The boys will go on their trip with Mrs Black. OK? And the girls will be with Mrs Farmer. You'll all have a great time, I'm sure.

Both groups are going to a museum – one to the Science Museum, that's the girls. The other group is going to the Transport Museum. You'll go to the museum you don't go to next week.

The boys will travel to their museum by bus, but the girls will use the train, as their museum is further away.

It's easier if the groups meet in different places. We'd like the boys to meet in the playground. Girls, please go to the school hall. Is that clear?

And you'll meet at different times too – nine fifteen and nine fifty. Girls, you should meet at the later time and boys at the earlier one.

At the beginning of both visits you'll have a talk by someone on the museum staff. Then you will have a tour of the museum. The girls' day will finish with a film, while the boys will have a quiz. So is that all clear? Has anyone got any questions?

PHOTOCOPIABLE ACTIVITIES: TEACHER'S NOTES GOLD experience 2ND EDITION A2

1A Four-in-a-row

AIM
- To practise free time vocabulary from the unit and review known vocabulary

ACTIVITY TYPE
Guessing game

CLASSROOM DYNAMICS
Pairwork

TIME TAKEN
10 minutes

WHEN TO USE
After Vocabulary: Free time, Exercise 3, page 15

PREPARATION
You will need one copy of the activity for each pair, and two different colours pens or pencils

PROCEDURE
1 Explain to students that they are going to play a game to practise new and known free time vocabulary. Elicit vocabulary learned in the previous level, e.g. *swimming, rollerblading, sailing, cycling, skiing.*
2 Divide the class into pairs.
3 Give each pair an activity sheet. Explain the rules. Students take it in turns to choose a square. They have around ten seconds to read the description and suggest a free time activity that matches. If they do this successfully, they colour the square. If they can't think of any within the ten seconds, then make a suggestion. If their suggestion doesn't fit the description, they cannot colour the square.
4 The object of the game is to colour four squares in a row. This can be vertical, horizontal or diagonal. The first student to do this is the winner.

ADAPTATION AND EXTENSION
- As an alternative, students can play the game in groups of four – made up of two pairs. Each pair chooses a square and work together to solve the clue.

ANSWER KEY
Possible answers:
1 painting/baking
2 camping/surfing
3 fishing/reading
4 sailing/swimming
5 reading/drawing
6 painting/reading
7 baking/skating
8 drawing/painting
9 camping/singing
10 skating/swimming
11 sailing/surfing
12 fishing/painting
13 rock climbing/surfing
14 skiing/camping
15 rollerblading/cycling
16 dancing/skiing

1B I never go shopping!

AIM
- To talk about free time activities using adverbs of frequency

ACTIVITY TYPE
Matching game

CLASSROOM DYNAMICS
Groups of four

TIME TAKEN
10 minutes

WHEN TO USE
After Vocabulary: Free time, Exercise 4, page 15 or as revision at the end of the unit

PREPARATION
You will need one copy of the activity for each group, cut up into cards.

PROCEDURE
1 Before the class: cut up one set of cards for each group – keep the free time collocations and adverbs of frequency in separate piles.
2 Divide the class into groups of four. If the class doesn't divide exactly, the game will still work with smaller groups.
3 Give each group their two piles of cards. Ask students to shuffle each pile and place them face down on the table.
4 Students take turns to pick up the top card from each pile. They make a grammatically correct sentence using the free time collocation and the adverb, e.g. 'I often go camping'.
5 The rest of the group decide whether they believe the sentence is true or not. If they decide the sentence is true, the student keeps the cards. If not, they return the cards to the bottom of the pile and play passes to the next player. Players must also return their cards to the pile if their sentence is not grammatically correct.
6 In order to the keep their cards, students should try to sound as convincing as possible, e.g. instead of saying 'I never watch YouTube videos', they could say 'I never watch YouTube videos before school'.
7 The player with the most cards at the end of the game is the winner.

ADAPTATION AND EXTENSION
- As an extension, ask students to use the cards to make predictions about how often their other classmates do the different activities, e.g. 'Emma always watches Youtube videos after school' or 'Marco sometimes plays the guitar'.
- Students read their questions for their classmates to say *True* or *False*.

PHOTOCOPIABLE ACTIVITIES: TEACHER'S NOTES GOLD experience 2ND EDITION A2

1C School clubs

AIM
- To extract information from texts

ACTIVITY TYPE
Information gap

CLASSROOM DYNAMICS
Pairwork

TIME TAKEN
10 minutes

WHEN TO USE
After Writing, Exercise 4, page 18

PREPARATION
You will need one copy of the activity for each pair, cut up into Student A/Student B worksheets.

PROCEDURE
1. Divide the class into pairs. Give each student a different worksheet.
2. Tell students they need to find the missing information about the clubs.
3. Students take it in turns to ask and answer questions using the *Word prompts* at the bottom of their sheets. Then they write the information in the correct places.
4. Fast finishers discuss the clubs in their pairs. They decide which one they would like to go to and explain why.

ANSWER KEY
Student A
1. Which day is baking club on?
2. How much is baking club?
3. Where is film club?
4. Who do/can I email about film club?

1 Tuesday 2 3 3 3A 4 Miss Rogers

Student B
1. When does baking club finish?
2. Where is baking club?
3. Which day is film club on?
4. How much is film club?

1 4.30 2 C4 3 Thursday 4 £2.50

ADAPTATION AND EXTENSION
- As a follow up, ask students to think of a different school club and make a notice for it.
- Divide the class into small groups. Students take turns to show their notice to the rest of the group and tell them about it, e.g. 'The skateboarding club is at 4.30 on Fridays. It's in the playground'.

2A Technology Bingo

AIM
- To practise technology vocabulary from the unit

ACTIVITY TYPE
Bingo game

CLASSROOM DYNAMICS
Groups of four

TIME TAKEN
10 minutes

WHEN TO USE
After Vocabulary: Technology, Exercise 8, page 27

PREPARATION
You will need one copy of the activity for each group, cut up into cards.

PROCEDURE
1. Divide the class into groups of four. Tell students that they are going to play a game of *Bingo*. Ask them to decide who wants to be the 'caller' in the game.
2. Give the caller the *Words* card and the other students a bingo grid. They should hold their grids so that no one else can see the pictures. Explain that the caller must read words in a random order. The other students listen and cross off the corresponding pictures on their cards.
3. The first person to cross off three pictures in a line is the winner.

ADAPTATION AND EXTENSION
- After students have finished the game, ask them to discuss the technology in their groups. They tell each other how many of the things in the pictures on their bingo grid they have at home and how often they use them.

PHOTOCOPIABLE ACTIVITIES: TEACHER'S NOTES

GOLD experience 2ND EDITION A2

2B Can you live without technology?

AIM
- To use the present simple and the present continuous to talk about different situations

ACTIVITY TYPE
Quiz

CLASSROOM DYNAMICS
Pairwork

TIME TAKEN
10–15 minutes

WHEN TO USE
After Listening, Exercise 6, page 28

PREPARATION
You will need one copy of the activity for each student.

PROCEDURE
1 Divide the class into pairs. Give each student an activity sheet. Explain that they are going to do a quiz to find out whether or not they can live without technology.
2 Students work together to complete the questions with the correct form of the verbs in brackets (present simple or present continuous).
3 Students take it in turns to ask and answer the questions. They mark their partner's answers on their activity sheet.
4 Students count how many As, Bs and Cs their partner has. They take it in turns to read the corresponding analysis to their partner.
5 Go through the activity with the class. Find out how many students couldn't live without technology.

ADAPTATION AND EXTENSION
- Discuss the activity with the class. Do students feel that they spend too much time texting/surfing the net/using social media? What are some positive things about technology? What are some negative things?

ANSWER KEY
1 're/are visiting 2 's/is talking 3 don't have/haven't got
4 're/are eating 5 see 6 're/are sleeping

2C Toby's computer lesson

AIM
- To extract information from texts

ACTIVITY TYPE
Cloze activity based in a photo

CLASSROOM DYNAMICS
Pairwork

TIME TAKEN
10 minutes

WHEN TO USE
After Exercise 9, page 31

PREPARATION
You will need one copy of the activity for each pair, with the Word cards cut up into cards.

PROCEDURE
1 Divide the class into pairs. Give each pair their photo, Word cards and the text.
2 Explain that students have to look at the picture and work together to complete the sentences about the picture with the correct words from the Word cards. They will use six words in total. There are six words they won't use.
3 Students work together to complete the task. Elicit answers during whole class feedback.

ANSWER KEY
1 's having
2 next to
3 enjoys
4 are learning
5 wants
6 's using

Not used: has, opposite, enjoying, learn, 's wanting, uses

ADAPTATION AND EXTENSION
- As an extension, ask students to work with their partner, taking it in turns to make their own sentences about the photo.

Photocopiable © Pearson Education Limited 2018

PHOTOCOPIABLE ACTIVITIES: TEACHER'S NOTES

GOLD experience 2ND EDITION **A2**

3A Collocation pairs

AIM
- To making collocations with vocabulary from the unit

ACTIVITY TYPE
Matching game

CLASSROOM DYNAMICS
Pairwork

TIME TAKEN
10 minutes

WHEN TO USE
After Vocabulary: school and education, Exercise 5, page 39

PREPARATION
You will need one copy of the activity for each pair, cut up into cards.

PROCEDURE
1 Divide the class into pairs and give each pair their cards, keeping the verbs and collocation endings separate. Ask students to shuffle the cards in their separate piles. Students then lay out the cards, face down in a 4 x 5 grid with verbs cards on the left and collocation endings on the right.
2 Student A picks up one card from the left-hand side of the grid and one from the right. If the two cards make a collocation, they keep them and have another go. If not, they turn them over again and play passes to Student B.
3 Students continue playing until all of the cards have been taken. The student with the most collocations at the end of the game is the winner.
4 Fast finishers take it in turns to make sentences with their collocations.

ADAPTATION AND EXTENSION
- As an alternative, this can be played as a game of *Snap!* Instead of laying out the cards in a grid, students keep the cards in their separate piles. One student takes each pile. Students take it in turns to put their card face up in the centre of the table. They continue until one card finishes a collocation from the preceding verb (e.g. *homework* follows *do*). The first student to shout *Snap!* collects all of the cards in the middle. The student with the most cards at the end of the game is the winner.

ANSWER KEY
Possible collocations:
get a good mark
get bored
have an exam / do an exam
have homework / do homework
learn a language
wear a school uniform
wear a football shirt
write on the board
write in your notebook
sit at a desk

3B Amy's day

AIM
- To practise past simple questions with *what, where, when* and *why*

ACTIVITY TYPE
Information gap

CLASSROOM DYNAMICS
Pairwork

TIME TAKEN
10 minutes

WHEN TO USE
After Speaking, Exercise 7, page 41

PREPARATION
You will need one copy of the activity for each pair, cut up into Student A/Student B worksheets.

PROCEDURE
1 Divide the class into pairs. Give each student a different half of the worksheet from their partner.
2 Tell students that they each have a story about a bad day with some information missing. They take it in turns to ask and answer questions using the *Word prompts* at the bottom of their sheets. They write the information in the correct places.
3 In their pairs, students read the completed version of their story.

ADAPTATION AND EXTENSION
- As a follow-up, ask students to think about a bad day they once had. In their pairs, students take turns telling each other about their day. Ask some of the students to share their story with the class.

ANSWER KEY
Student A
1 What time did Amy wake up?
2 How did she travel to school?
3 What was her first lesson?
4 When did she meet Nathan?
5 What did Amy look at?
6 What did Amy and Nathan do?
1 eight o'clock 2 walked 3 physics 4 lunchtime 5 feet 6 laughed

Student B
1 What did Amy do after she put on her uniform?
2 What time did Amy arrive at school?
3 What happened in the physics lesson?
4 Where did Amy meet Nathan?
5 What did Amy tell Nathan about?
6 What did Amy see?
1 she cleaned her teeth 2 8.30 3 a test 4 school café
5 her morning 6 blue shoe

PHOTOCOPIABLE ACTIVITIES: TEACHER'S NOTES

GOLD experience 2ND EDITION A2

3C A fun day

AIM
- To make sentences about free time activities with adverbs of frequency

To use sequencing words to order events

ACTIVITY TYPE
Ordering a story

CLASSROOM DYNAMICS
Pairwork

TIME TAKEN
10 minutes

WHEN TO USE
After Writing, Exercise 3, page 42

PREPARATION
You will need one copy of the activity for each pair, cut up into cards.

PROCEDURE
1 Divide the class into pairs. Hand out the cards and ask students to shuffle them.
2 Give each pair a pile of shuffled strips.
3 Students work together to put the strips of paper into the correct order to make a story. They use the sequencing words along with the information on the paper to help them order the events.

ANSWER KEY
See worksheet

ADAPTATION AND EXTENSION
- For a livelier activity, ask students to work in teams. In a class of thirty, divide the class into two groups of fifteen. Give fourteen students a piece of paper. Tell students that they must read their sentences and stand in the correct order to recreate the story. The remaining student helps the rest of the group to organise themselves. In a class of more than thirty, have more than one 'helper' for each team. In a class of fewer than thirty, divide the story into fewer than fourteen parts, by leaving some sentences together.

4A Shopping definitions

AIM
- To revise shopping vocabulary

ACTIVITY TYPE
Definitions quiz

CLASSROOM DYNAMICS
Pairwork

TIME TAKEN
5–10 minutes

WHEN TO USE
After Vocabulary: shopping, Exercise 6, page 51

PREPARATION
You will need one copy of the activity for each pair, cut up into Student A/Student B worksheets.

PROCEDURE
1 Divide the class into pairs. Give each student a different half of the worksheet from their partner.
2 Explain that students are going to do a quiz in their pairs. They each have four definitions with the answer in brackets. They take turns reading the definitions for their partner to give the correct answer from the word pool at the bottom of their sheet.
3 Students do the quiz, awarding themselves one point for each correct answer. The student with the most points at the end is the winner. If both students have the same amount of points, there is a draw.
4 Go through the activity with the class. Elicit the correct answers from students.

ADAPTATION AND EXTENSION
- Make the quiz more challenging for confident students by cutting off the word pool at the bottom of each half.
- With less confident students, use the activity as a non-competitive game rather than a quiz. Students can help each other by giving clues if their partner is stuck, e.g. 'It begins with a *b*./It has two words'.

ANSWER KEY
See worksheet

Photocopiable © Pearson Education Limited 2018   183

PHOTOCOPIABLE ACTIVITIES: TEACHER'S NOTES

GOLD experience 2ND EDITION **A2**

4B Which shop?

AIM
- To use comparative and superlative adjectives to explain choices

ACTIVITY TYPE
Group discussion

CLASSROOM DYNAMICS
Groups of four

TIME TAKEN
15–20 minutes

WHEN TO USE
After Listening, Exercise 5, page 52

PREPARATION
You will need one copy of the activity for each group, with the *Shopping cards* cut up into cards.

PROCEDURE
1 Tell students they are going to do an activity about comparing different shops and shopping experiences. Review adjectives they might need to describe the shops and shopping experiences, e.g. *cheap, expensive, big, interesting, good, nice, friendly, busy.*
2 Divide the class into groups of four. Give each group a copy of the activity. Allow five minutes for students to read through the reviews in their groups.
3 Give each group a set of shopping cards. Ask them to choose one sports item and one clothing item each.
4 Explain that students must decide which shops they are going to buy their items from and explain their choices to the rest of the group, using comparative and superlative adjectives, e.g. *I'm going to buy my jeans from Suki's Store. It's the most expensive shop, but the shopping experience is better.*
5 Set a time limit of fifteen minutes, and begin the activity. Monitor and help students as necessary, making a note of things to discuss during whole class feedback.
6 When the time is up, ask each group to share some of their choices with the class. Complete whole class feedback.

ADAPTATION AND EXTENSION
- Discuss the shops as a class. Ask students what they like / dislike about each one. Take a vote to find the favourite clothes shop and sports shop.

4C Can you tell me the way?

AIM
- To review phrases for asking for directions and giving directions

ACTIVITY TYPE
Dialogue

CLASSROOM DYNAMICS
Pairwork

TIME TAKEN
10 minutes

WHEN TO USE
After Speaking, Exercise 6, page 53

PREPARATION
You will need one copy of the activity for each pair, with the white cards cut up into cards.

PROCEDURE
1 Divide the class into pairs. Give each pair a gray activity sheet and a set of white cards.
2 Students take it in turns to read a sentence or question from the gray activity sheet, and their partner must find the correct response from the white cards.
3 Go through the activity with the class and elicit the correct answers.
4 Students keep taking turns until the conversation is complete.

ANSWER KEY
See worksheet

ADAPTATION AND EXTENSION
- Fast finishers practise the conversation, changing details, e.g. shops, directions, bus number

PHOTOCOPIABLE ACTIVITIES: TEACHER'S NOTES GOLD experience 2ND EDITION **A2**

5A Film reviews

AIM
- To give opinions about different films using vocabulary from the unit

ACTIVITY TYPE
Survey

CLASSROOM DYNAMICS
Groups of six

TIME TAKEN
10–15 minutes

WHEN TO USE
After Vocabulary: Entertainment, Exercise 5, page 63

PREPARATION
You will need one copy of the activity for each group.

PROCEDURE
1 Divide the class into groups of six. If the class doesn't divide exactly, the activity will still work with smaller groups.
2 Give each group a copy of the activity. Tell students that they are going to give their opinions on different films. In their groups, ask students to think of a film for each of the film categories on the left. They write the names of the films on the activity sheet.
3 Students take turns asking someone in their group about a film on the list. Their classmate gives the film a rating (from one to five stars) and chooses an adjective that describes it. The first student records this information by shading the appropriate number of stars and ticking the box of the chosen adjective. In a group of six, each person 'reviews' one film. In a smaller group, some students can review more than one film.
4 Ask each group to share some of their reviews. Elicit some reasons for their choices.

ADAPTATION AND EXTENSION
- As an alternative, this can be done as a mingling activity. Ask students to choose a film for each category and walk around the room, finding different people to talk to. They take it in turns to choose a film and ask their classmate to review it in the way described in step 3.

5B Interruptions!

AIM
- To make sentences with the past continuous and the past simple

ACTIVITY TYPE
Matching game

CLASSROOM DYNAMICS
Groups of four

TIME TAKEN
15 minutes

WHEN TO USE
After Listening, Exercise 6, page 64

PREPARATION
You will need one copy of the activity for each group, cut up into cards.

PROCEDURE
1 Divide the class into groups of four. Give each group a set of cards. Explain that there are two types of cards in each set: *Situation* cards (grey) and *Interruption* cards (white). Tell students that they are going to use the cards to make sentences with the past simple and past continuous.
2 Ask students to shuffle the cards and lay them out face down in a four by five grid.
3 Students take turns to pick up two cards. If they pick up one *Situation* card and one *Interruption* card, they make a sentence about the two events, e.g. 'While I was having a bath, the police arrived'. If the sentence is grammatically correct, they keep the cards.
4 If students pick up two *Situation* cards or two *Interruption* cards, they turn them over again without speaking and play passes to the next person.
5 The winner is the person with the most cards at the end of the game.

ADAPTATION AND EXTENSION
- For a less challenging activity, ask students to work in pairs. Give Student A a pile of *Situation cards* and Student B a pile of *Interruption cards*. Each student picks up the first card from their pile. They work together to make the sentence, e.g. '*While I was walking to school … an elephant escaped!*'

PHOTOCOPIABLE ACTIVITIES: TEACHER'S NOTES   GOLD experience 2ND EDITION **A2**

5C Film night

ACTIVITY TYPE
Information gap

EXAM LINK
A communicative adaptation of KEY for Schools Reading and Writing Part 4. In the exam, students will choose *Right*, *Wrong* or *Don't know* for each sentence and circle the corresponding letter.

CLASSROOM DYNAMICS
Pairwork

TIME TAKEN
10 minutes

WHEN TO USE
After Writing, Exercise 12, page 67

PREPARATION
You will need one copy of the activity for each pair, cut up into Student A/Student B worksheets.

PROCEDURE
1. Divide the class into pairs. Give each a different worksheet from their partner.
2. Ask students to read the story and the *True or False?* sentences on their worksheet.
3. Explain that students have to find the missing information by taking turns to read the sentences to their partners. If the sentence is true, they put a tick in the box and complete the information in the story. If the sentence is false, their partner must correct it, e.g. A: 'As the film was ending, Libby arrived.' B: 'False. Libby arrived as the film was beginning'. Students put a cross in the box and add the correct information to the story.

ADAPTATION AND EXTENSION
- For further practice of the language from the Student's Book lesson (see the *explore language* box at the top of page 67), ask students to read the full story after they have completed the task. They underline all of the phrases that tell us when something happened (*Last Friday; At the beginning of the evening; A few minutes later; At the end of the evening*).

ANSWER KEY
Student A
1 True
2 False. As the film was beginning, Libby arrived.
3 False. Violet thought the film was awesome.
4 False. At the end of the evening, Violet's brother did the washing up

Student B
1 False. While dad was phoning the restaurant, Violet and her brother chose the film.
2 True
3 False. Libby's brother fell asleep while he was watching the film.
4 False. At the end of the evening, Violet tidied the room.

6A Our travel plans

AIM
- To use *will* and *going to* to ask and answer about travel plans

ACTIVITY TYPE
Information gap

CLASSROOM DYNAMICS
Pairwork

TIME TAKEN
10 minutes

WHEN TO USE
After Grammar: talking about the future, Exercise 7, page 74

PREPARATION
You will need one copy of the activity for each pair, cut up into Student A/Student B worksheets.

PROCEDURE
1. Tell students they are going to talk about people's travel plans. Review the use of *going to* and *will*. Establish that we use *going to* for intentions and *will* for things we know, e.g. *The weather will be hot; The journey will take four hours.*
2. Divide the class into pairs. Give each student a different half of the worksheet from their partner.
3. Tell students they each have information about three different people's travel plans. They take it in turns to ask and answer questions to find the missing information.
4. Students use the question prompts at the bottom of their worksheet to help them ask questions about the first two people. Then, they use the same question forms to ask about the third person. They write the missing information in the correct places.
5. Go through the activity with the class. Elicit the correct answers. Elicit what travel plans students find most interesting and why.

ADAPTATION AND EXTENSION
- As a follow up, ask students to pretend they are planning a trip to another country. They make notes for each of the headings on the worksheet (*country, travel by, weather, travel time*). In their pairs, students take turns to ask and answer about their trips.

ANSWER KEY
Student A
1 Australia 2 two days 3 train 4 cold 5 Brazil 6 hot

Student B
1 plane 2 warm 3 Russia 4 six days 5 plane 6 four hours

PHOTOCOPIABLE ACTIVITIES: TEACHER'S NOTES

6B Travel dominoes

AIM
- To practise collocations for travelling

ACTIVITY TYPE
Domino game

CLASSROOM DYNAMICS
Pairwork

TIME TAKEN
10 minutes

WHEN TO USE
After Vocabulary: travel and transport, Exercise 7, page 75

PREPARATION
You will need one copy of the activity for each pair, cut up into domino cards.

PROCEDURE
1 Elicit rules for travel collocations:
   We can go *on* foot (but not on bus, plane, train, etc.).
   We can go *by* car, train, bus or any other types of vehicle.
   We can take, catch or get any type of transport that you need a ticket for.
   We can use *travel by* … with any form of transport.
   We can *arrive at* any place.
2 Divide the class into pairs. Give each pair a set of dominoes.
3 Ask students to shuffle and deal out the dominoes equally.
4 Players take turns putting down dominoes. The first part of each domino must complete the collocation from the one before.
5 If a player can't complete a collocation, they miss a go and their partner has another turn.
6 The game continues until all of the dominoes have been put down.

ADAPTATION AND EXTENSION
- As an alternative, ask students to deal out only ten of the dominoes, so that they have five each. They lay out the rest of the cards face down on the table. Students take turns to put down their dominoes. If they can't make a collocation, they pick up a card from table and their partner has a go. The first student to put down all of their dominoes is the winner.

6C A great trip

AIM
- To extract information from texts

ACTIVITY TYPE
Matching activity

CLASSROOM DYNAMICS
Pairwork

TIME TAKEN
10 minutes

WHEN TO USE
After Writing, Exercise 3, page 78

PREPARATION
You will need one copy of the activity for each pair, with the *Adverts* cut up into cards.

PROCEDURE
1 Divide the class into pairs. Give each pair an email and a set of adverts.
2 Ask students to work in pairs to read the activity sheet and find the advert that matches the place or attraction from each paragraph of the email (1–6).
3 Check answers as a class and elicit which trips students would most like to go on and why.

ADAPTATION AND EXTENSION
- As a follow-up, ask students to plan their own day trip to London, choosing from the different transport, places and activities in the adverts.
- As an extension, ask students to look at the six adverts they didn't use for the main activity. They work in pairs or small groups to create an email about the attractions. Monitor and help students as needed. Ask groups to share their ideas with the class during whole class feedback.

ANSWER KEY
Paragraph 1: Express trains
Paragraph 2: Prince Lane Apartment
Paragraph 3: See the city by speedboat!
Paragraph 4: Park Café
Paragraph 5: Films in the park
Paragraph 6: Classical concert

PHOTOCOPIABLE ACTIVITIES: TEACHER'S NOTES

GOLD experience 2ND EDITION **A2**

7A Could you ride a bike?

AIM
- To ask and answer questions about present and past abilities

ACTIVITY TYPE
Survey

CLASSROOM DYNAMICS
Whole class

TIME TAKEN
10 minutes

WHEN TO USE
After Grammar: ability and possibility, Exercise 6, page 86

PREPARATION
You will need one copy of the activity for each student.

PROCEDURE
1. Tell students they are going to talk to other people in the class about their abilities.
2. Give each student a copy of the activity. Ask students to choose two more skills and add them to the chart.
3. Draw attention to the examples in speech bubbles at the bottom of the activity sheet. Tell students they will use these question types to ask about people's abilities now and in the past.
4. Ask students to walk around the class, choosing a different person to ask about each skill. They write the name of the person in the left-hand column and ask questions using the structures in the examples. Students write the answers in the chart.
5. Go through the activity with the class. Ask different students to share some of their findings.

ADAPTATION AND EXTENSION
- To minimise disruption, this activity can be done small groups. Students take turns asking and talking to different members of their group. At the end of the activity, ask one student from each group to report back to the class.

7B In a spin

AIM
- To practise sports collocations with *play, go* and *do*

ACTIVITY TYPE
Collocation game

CLASSROOM DYNAMICS
Pairwork

TIME TAKEN
10 minutes

WHEN TO USE
After Vocabulary: sports and equipment, Exercise 6, page 87

PREPARATION
You will need one copy of the activity for each pair, with the *Spinner* cut out and the *Word cards* cut up into cards, and a pencil.

PROCEDURE
1. Tell students they are going to play a game to practise collocations for sport with *play, go* and *do*. Give each pair a spinner and a set of word cards.
2. Ask students to put a pencil though the middle of the spinner. They shuffle and lay out the word cards on the table, face up, so the words can easily be seen.
3. Students take turns to spin the spinner and read the verb. They find a sports activity to go with the verb and make a sentence, e.g. 'I play badminton every Tuesday'.
4. If the sentence is correct, the student keeps the card. If it is incorrect, or if they can't find a match, play passes to their partner.
5. The student with the most cards at the end of the game is the winner.

ADAPTATION AND EXTENSION
- For a more challenging game, do not use the *Word cards*. Tell students they are each going to spin the spinner seven times. Students take it in turns to spin the spinner, read the verb and complete the collocation with an activity of their own. They get one point for each collocation, but they cannot repeat the same collocation on a different turn.

PHOTOCOPIABLE ACTIVITIES: TEACHER'S NOTES — GOLD experience 2ND EDITION A2

7C Find the answers

AIM
- To use grammar and context to match questions with answers

ACTIVITY TYPE
Matching activity

CLASSROOM DYNAMICS
Individual and pairwork

TIME TAKEN
10 minutes

WHEN TO USE
After Speaking, Exercise 4, page 89

PREPARATION
You will need one copy of the activity for each pair.

PROCEDURE
1 Divide the class into pairs. Give each pair an activity sheet.
2 Students work together to read the questions on the left and find the correct answers on the right. They draw lines to match the questions to the answers.
3 Ask students to compare their answers with another pair. They make changes to their own answers if necessary.
4 Go through the activity with the class. Elicit the correct answers from students.

ADAPTATION AND EXTENSION
- For a more challenging activity, cut the activity sheet in half lengthways to separate the questions from the answers. Give the questions to one student in each pair, and the answers to the other. Ask students to read through their halves of the activity sheet without showing their partners. Students work together to match the questions and answers; Student A read the question and Student B finds the correct answer and responds with it.

ANSWER KEY
1 D 2 F 3 B 4 E 5 A 6 C

8A Which animal?

AIM
- To practise vocabulary from the unit

ACTIVITY TYPE
Guessing game

CLASSROOM DYNAMICS
Groups of six

TIME TAKEN
10–15 minutes

WHEN TO USE
After Listening, Exercise 4, page 100

PREPARATION
You will need one copy of the activity for each group, cut up into cards.

PROCEDURE
1 Tell students they are going to play a guessing game about animals. Some of the animal words are from the lesson; others are one students have learned about previously.
2 Review vocabulary. Make sure that the words *kangaroo, penguin, snake, bear, camel* and *monkey* are elicited. Before starting, teach the word *fur*.
3 Divide the class into groups of six. If the class doesn't divide equally, include some smaller groups.
4 Give each group a pile of cards, face down. (With smaller groups, give one card per student.) Students each take a card without showing it to the others in their group. They solve the anagrams and write the missing words.
5 Students take turns to read their cards for the rest of the group to guess the animal. The group that guesses all of the animals first is the winner.

ADAPTATION AND EXTENSION
- As an extension, ask students to make their own animal descriptions for the group to guess.

ANSWER KEY

A kangaroo	1 Australia	2 dry	3 sun
B penguin	1 coast	2 snow	3 ice
C snake	1 rainforest	2 hot	3 cold
D bear	1 Europe	2 warm	3 storm
E camel	1 desert	2 boiling	3 freezing
F monkey	1 Antarctica	2 island	3 hot

PHOTOCOPIABLE ACTIVITIES: TEACHER'S NOTES

GOLD experience 2ND EDITION **A2**

8B Have you ever … ?

AIM
- To use the ask and answer questions using the present perfect with *ever*

ACTIVITY TYPE
Matching game

CLASSROOM DYNAMICS
Pairwork

TIME TAKEN
10 minutes

WHEN TO USE
After Listening, Exercise 6, page 100

PREPARATION
You will need one copy of the activity for each pair, cut up into cards.

PROCEDURE
1. Divide the class into pairs. Give each pair a set of cards. Ask students to spread the cards face up on the table.
2. Students work together to make eight sensible questions with the cards. They then take it in turns to ask and answer the questions.
3. Go through the activity with the class. Check the questions and ask different students for their responses.

ADAPTATION AND EXTENSION
- As an extension, students ask students to do a survey in groups. They write down the questions and find out how many people have done each thing. Alternatively, students can come up with their own questions.

ANSWER KEY
See worksheet

8C Holiday messages

AIM
- To complete and compare messages about holidays

ACTIVITY TYPE
Cloze activity

CLASSROOM DYNAMICS
Individual and pairwork

TIME TAKEN
10 minutes

WHEN TO USE
After Writing, Exercise 8, page 103

PREPARATION
You will need one copy of the activity for each student or pair.

PROCEDURE
1. Tell students they are going to do an activity involving messages from different holidays.
2. Give one activity sheet to each student. Ask them to read the messages and complete each one with the correct words from the wordpool.
3. Go through the answers with the class.
4. Ask students to read the messages again and decide which one sounds better and why. Establish that Becky's message sounds better because it has a more interesting variety of adjectives. She uses *really, very* and *a bit* to modify adjectives. She uses stronger adjectives than Alex. (Becky uses *amazing, fantastic* and *love*; Dan uses *nice, good* and *like*). Becky also uses friendly language.
5. Ask students to make suggestions about how Alex could make his message more interesting.

ADAPTATION AND EXTENSION
- As a lead in or a discussion after the activity, ask students what kind of messages they send to friends and family when they are away from home, e.g. text messages, social media posts, emails, postcards. What kind of information to they like to share?
- Allow less confident students to work together to complete the messages.

ANSWER KEY
Becky's message
1 fantastic 2 very 3 amazing 4 love 5 bit

Alex's message
1 apartment 2 too 3 view 4 sea 5 scared

PHOTOCOPIABLE ACTIVITIES: TEACHER'S NOTES

GOLD experience 2ND EDITION A2

9A All mixed up

AIM
- To review food vocabulary from the unit

ACTIVITY TYPE
Substituting words in dialogues

CLASSROOM DYNAMICS
Pairwork

TIME TAKEN
10–15 minutes

WHEN TO USE
After Vocabulary: food and health, Exercise 6, page 111

PREPARATION
You will need one copy of the activity for each pair.

PROCEDURE
1 Before you start the activity, review food vocabulary from the lesson. Ask students go give examples of different foods you can bake, barbecue, boil, fry, grill and roast. Point out that we can have boiled, baked and roast potatoes, but we don't usually say 'fried potatoes'; we say 'chips' or 'fries'. Elicit the word *sauce* from the previous level. Ask questions, e.g. 'What do we have on pasta?'
2 Divide the class into pairs. Give each pair an activity sheet. Explain that the bold words have been mixed up and are in the wrong places. Students work together to replace each word in bold with the correct word from another dialogue.
3 Go through the answers with the class.
4 Ask students to practise the dialogues in their pairs.

ADAPTATION AND EXTENSION
- This activity can also be done in groups of six. Before the lesson, cut the activity sheet into separate conversations. Give each student a conversation and ask them to think about which words they could substitute for the ones in bold. Students ask the other members in their group if they have any of the words they are looking for. Once students have completed their own conversation, they help others in the group to complete theirs.
- As an extension, ask students to work in pairs. They choose one of the conversations and continue it.

ANSWER KEY
1 chips 2 fried 3 cereal 4 baked 5 pasta 6 sauce 7 salad 8 boiled 9 barbecued 10 sandwich 11 cake 12 biscuits

9B What should I do?

AIM
- To give advice using *should* and *shouldn't*

ACTIVITY TYPE
Discussion

CLASSROOM DYNAMICS
Groups of three or four

TIME TAKEN
10 minutes

WHEN TO USE
After Listening, Exercise 6, page 112

PREPARATION
You will need one copy of the activity for each group, cut up into cards.

PROCEDURE
1 Divide the class into groups of three. If the class doesn't divide exactly, the game will work with pairs or groups of four. Give each group a set of cards. Ask students to shuffle them and place them face down on the table.
2 Set a time limit of ten minutes. Students take it in turns to pick up a card and read the problem. The other students in the group give advice about what they should or shouldn't do, e.g. A: 'I'm worried about my English test.' B: 'You should talk to your teacher'
3 Go through the activity with the class. Ask each group to share some of the advice that people gave.

ADAPTATION AND EXTENSION
- This game can also be played as a mingling activity. Give each student a card and set a time limit of ten minutes. Students walk around the class and choose a partner. They take it in turns to read their cards and give advice. Students then swap cards with their partner and find another student to talk to. They continue in this way until the time is up.

PHOTOCOPIABLE ACTIVITIES: TEACHER'S NOTES

GOLD experience 2ND EDITION A2

9C The race

ACTIVITY TYPE
- To review conjunctions from the unit

SKILLS FOCUS
Using and *because* and *so* to link and contrast ideas in a story

CLASSROOM DYNAMICS
Pairwork

TIME TAKEN
10 minutes

WHEN TO USE
After Writing, Exercise 11, page 115

PREPARATION
You will need one copy of the activity for each pair.

PROCEDURE
1 Divide the class into pairs. Give each pair a copy of the activity sheet. Explain that students have a story with conjunctions missing. Teach them term *broken leg*.
2 Ask students read the story and complete each gap with *and*, *but*, *so* or *because*.
3 Go through the answers with the class.

ADAPTATION AND EXTENSION
- For a more challenging activity, cut the story along the lines, discarding the numbers. Ask students to complete the gaps and then put the sentences in order.
- As an extension, ask students to look at the sentences with *so* and *because* again. Ask them to rewrite them using the opposite conjunction, e.g. *Aisha wanted to help her friend, so she stopped running = Aisha stopped running because she wanted to help her friend.*

ANSWER KEY
1 and 2 because 3 but 4 so 5 and 6 so 7 because 8 but

1A FOUR-IN-A-ROW

1 You can do this inside.	2 This is better in warm weather.	3 You can sit down to do this.	4 You do this in water.
5 You can do this at school.	6 You can do this in any weather.	7 You can do this alone.	8 You need paper for this.
9 You usually do this with your family.	10 You need special clothes for this.	11 It's not a good idea to do this at night.	12 This is a quiet hobby.
13 This can be dangerous.	14 You can only do this outside.	15 You do this on wheels.	16 This is good exercise.

baking   camping   cycling   dancing   drawing   fishing   painting   reading
rock climbing   rollerblading   sailing   singing   skating   skiing   surfing   swimming

1B I NEVER GO SHOPPING!

go shopping	always
play football	usually
play the guitar	normally
watch videos	often
play the guitar	sometimes
go on a sleepover	don't often
go to the cinema	don't usually
listen to music	never

1C SCHOOL CLUBS

Student A

Baking club

Make delicious cakes, biscuits and bread at Baking club.
We meet every ¹ ....
3.30–4.30, Room C4
²£ .... per person

Make your own film!

Come to Film club!
Every Thursday at lunchtime
Room ³ ....
£2.50 per week
Please email ⁴ .... to join!

Word prompts

1 Which day / baking club?
2 How much / baking club?
3 Where / film club?
4 Who / email about film club?

Student B

Baking club

We meet every Tuesday
3.30– ¹ ....
Room ² ....
£3 per person

Make your own film!

Come to Film club every
³ .... at lunchtime
Room 3A
⁴ .... per week
Please email Miss Rogers to join!

Word prompts

1 When / baking club finish?
2 Where / baking club?
3 Which day / film club?
4 How much / film club?

2A TECHNOLOGY BINGO

Words

Read these in any order, but remember to tick each one.

- app ☐
- digital camera ☐
- headphones ☐
- keyboard ☐
- laptop ☐
- mobile phone ☐
- mouse ☐
- printer ☐
- screen ☐
- speakers ☐
- tablet ☐
- webcam ☐

2B CAN YOU LIVE WITHOUT TECHNOLOGY?

1 You .... (visit) an old friend. What are you doing?
   A We're chatting. We've got lots to talk about.
   B We're taking photos on our phones.
   C We're texting other people.

2 Your mum .... (talk) about to you about school. What are you doing?
   A I'm listening.
   B I'm thinking about other things.
   C I'm texting my friend.

3 You're on holiday and you .... (not have) an internet connection. How do you feel?
   A It's not a problem. I'm too busy having fun to use my phone.
   B I'm a bit disappointed. I wanted to use my phone to find out about places to visit.
   C I'm really upset! I can't surf the internet or use social media. I want to go home!

4 You .... (eat) dinner. What else is happening?
   A I'm talking to my family.
   B I'm listening to music.
   C I'm surfing the net.

5 You .... (see) a photo of your friend at a cool party on social media. What do you think?
   A I'm glad my friend had a good time.
   B I'm not happy. Why didn't I get an invitation to the party?
   C I'm not happy. Now I need to upload twenty pictures of cool things that I'm doing.

6 It's 10 p.m. You .... (sleep). Where's your phone?
   A downstairs.
   B in my bedroom – but it isn't on
   C next to my bed – and it's on

What your score says about you

Mostly As

You can definitely live without technology! It's good that you don't spend too much time on your phone or online, but it's OK to use technology sometimes.

Mostly Bs

You like technology, but there are lots of other things in your life. You have time for friends, sports and hobbies. Well done!

Mostly Cs

You can't live without technology – or so you think! You should try to take a break. The real world can be exciting, too!

2C TOBY'S COMPUTER LESSON

1 This morning, Toby .... a computer lesson at school.

2 He's sitting .... his friend, Mia.

3 He always .... learning about technology.

4 In this lesson, the students .... how to make a website.

5 Toby .... his website to be interesting.

6 He .... lots of pictures and photos.

Word cards

| 's having | has | enjoys | enjoying | wants | 's wanting |
| next to | opposite | learn | are learning | uses | 's using |

3A COLLOCATION PAIRS

get	do	a good mark	homework
get	have	bored	exam
wear	write	a school uniform	on the board
wear	write	a football shirt	in your notebook
learn	sit	a language	at a desk

PHOTOCOPIABLE ACTIVITIES GOLD experience 2ND EDITION **A2**

3B AMY'S DAY

Student A

Amy woke up at **1** .... She was late! She put on her uniform and then cleaned her teeth. There wasn't time for breakfast!
Amy **2** .... to school very quickly! She arrived at school at 8.30 – just on time! Her first lesson was **3** .... (not her favourite subject!) and this morning there was a test.
At **4** .... Amy met her friend, Nathan, in the school café. Amy told Nathan about her morning. 'I'm having a bad day, too,' Nathan said. 'I got dressed too quickly – look!' Amy looked at Nathan's **5** .... She saw one blue shoe and one black shoe. Amy and Nathan **6** ....

1 What time / Amy wake up?
2 How / she / travel to school?
3 What / first lesson?
4 When / she / meet Nathan?
5 What / Amy / look at?
6 What Amy and Nathan / do?

---- ✂ --

Student B

Amy woke up at eight o'clock. She was late! She put on her uniform and then **1** .... There wasn't time for breakfast!
Amy walked to school very quickly. She arrived at school at **2** .... – just on time! Her first lesson was physics (not her favourite subject!) and this morning there was **3** ....
At lunchtime, Amy met her best friend, Nathan, in the **4** .... Amy told Nathan about **5** .... 'I'm having a bad day, too,' Nathan said, 'I got dressed too quickly – look!' Amy looked at Nathan's feet. She saw one black shoe and one **6** .... Amy and Nathan laughed.

1 Why / Amy / do / after she put on her uniform?
2 What time / Amy arrive / at school?
3 What happen / in physics lesson?
4 Where / Amy / meet Nathan?
5 What / Amy / tell Nathan about?
6 What / Amy / see?

Photocopiable © Pearson Education Limited 2018

3C A FUN DAY

Today, we had an activity day at school. It was great!

First, we did a puzzle in teams.

The puzzle had lots of different coloured shapes.

We worked together to make a picture from the shapes.

When we finished the puzzle, we had lunch.

At lunchtime, we had a picnic in the school field.

I had sandwiches, an apple and some cake – yum!

After lunch, there was a sports competition.

I played table tennis in the competition.

I didn't win any of the matches, but it was fun.

At the end of the day, there were prizes.

I got a prize for working well in a team.

When I got home, I showed my prize to my sister.

Now she wants to have an activity day, too!

4A SHOPPING DEFINITIONS

Student A

something for sale at a very cheap price	(bargain)
to put on clothes in a shop before you buy them	(try on)
you can spend this in the USA	(dollar)
to keep your money until you can buy the thing(s) you want	(save)

cash department store pay receipt

Student B

coins or paper money (not cards)	(cash)
to give money to buy something	(pay)
a piece of paper you get when you buy something	(receipt)
a big shop that sells lots of different things	(department store)

bargain dollar save try on

4B WHICH SHOP?

Clothes shops

Suki's Store	Fashion 1	Main Street Market
Cost £££££	**Cost** ££££££	**Cost** £££££
Shopping experience ★★★★☆	**Shopping experience** ★★☆☆☆	**Shopping experience** ★★★☆☆
'This shop is amazing! The clothes are so cool and there are smart mirrors in the changing rooms!' 'The shop is very small and the clothes are too expensive.'	'I buy all my clothes here. They look good and they're not too expensive.' 'The shop assistants are never friendly or helpful. Don't go!'	'This market is really big! You can find anything you want.' 'It's busy and horrible here!'

Sports Shops

Sports 2 Go	Smart Sports	Sports Online
Cost £££££	**Cost** £££££	**Cost** £££££
Shopping experience ★☆☆☆☆	**Shopping experience** ★★★☆☆	**Shopping experience** ★★★★☆
'Everything's a bargain here. I love it!' 'There are lots of customers, but there aren't many shop assistants. Awful!'	'It's a lovely shop. The shop assistants really helpful.' 'It's too far out of town.'	'Why go shopping when you can shop online? It's so easy.' 'My trainers took three weeks to arrive!'

Shopping cards

football	tennis racket	skipping rope	surfboard
jeans	T-shirt	socks	sunglasses

4C CAN YOU TELL ME THE WAY?

A: Excuse me, can you tell me the way to the department store, please?	B: There are two department stores in town. Do you want Green's or Rachel's?
A: Which is the nearest?	B: Well, Green's is the nearest, but it's more expensive than Rachel's.
A: Oh dear. I don't want to spend a lot of money. How far is it to Rachel's?	B: It takes about twenty minutes to walk there from here.
A: That's a long time!	B: Yes, it is. But you can get the bus. That's much quicker.
A: Good idea! Which bus do I need?	B: You need bus number twenty-nine.
A: And where can I catch the bus?	B: The bus stop is just there by the bridge. Can you see it?
A: Oh, yes! Thank you. Where do I get off the bus?	B: Get off the bus just after the cinema and then go straight on. Rachel's is opposite the museum.
A: That's great. Thank you for your help.	B: You're welcome!

5A FILM REVIEWS

science fiction	romantic	horror	documentary	comedy	animated	action	Film name
☆☆☆☆☆	☆☆☆☆☆	☆☆☆☆☆	☆☆☆☆☆	☆☆☆☆☆	☆☆☆☆☆	☆☆☆☆☆	Rating
☐	☐	☐	☐	☐	☐	☐	**awesome**
☐	☐	☐	☐	☐	☐	☐	**great**
☐	☐	☐	☐	☐	☐	☐	**funny**
☐	☐	☐	☐	☐	☐	☐	**strange**
☐	☐	☐	☐	☐	☐	☐	**terrible**

5B INTERRUPTIONS!

having a bath	visiting the zoo	watching TV	surfing the internet	playing football
skiing	reading book	sleeping	travelling to school	shopping
phone / ring	elephant / escape	police / arrive	my computer / break	my friend / text
I / see / famous person	I / find / money	I / hear / loud noise	I / fall over	I / meet / friend

5C FILM NIGHT

Student A

My Film Night
by Violet

Last Friday, I had a film night at my house. It was great!

At the beginning of the evening, my brother and I ¹.................................... . While dad was phoning the restaurant, my brother and I chose the film. We decided to watch *Wonder*.

As the film was ²...................................., my cousin, Libby arrived. She sat next to me on the sofa.

A few minutes later, there was a knock on the door. Our pizzas were here! Libby shared my pizza. It was delicious.

I thought the film was ³...................................., but my brother thought it was boring. He fell asleep while we were watching it!

At the end of the evening, I tidied the room and my brother ⁴.................................... . Next week, we're going to have a film night at Libby's house.

True or False?
1 At the beginning of the evening, Violet and her brother chose pizzas. ☐
2 As the film was ending, Libby arrived. ☐
3 Violet thought the film was OK. ☐
4 At the end of the evening, Violet's brother had a bath. ☐

Student B

My Film Night
by Violet

Last Friday, I had a film night at my house. It was great!

At the beginning of the evening, we chose pizzas. While dad was ¹.................................... the restaurant, my brother and I chose the film. We decided to watch *Wonder*.

As the film was beginning, my cousin, Libby arrived. She sat next to me on the sofa.

A few minutes later, there was a knock on the door. Our pizzas were here! ².................................... shared my pizza. It was delicious.

I thought the film was awesome, but my brother thought it was boring. He ³.................................... while we were watching it!

At the end of the evening, I ⁴.................................... and my brother did the washing up. Next week, we're going to have a film night at Libby's house.

True or False?
1 While dad was texting the restaurant, Violet and her brother chose the film. ☐
2 Libby shared Violet's pizza. ☐
3 Libby's brother phoned a friend while he was watching the film. ☐
4 At the end of the evening, Violet had a snack. ☐

PHOTOCOPIABLE ACTIVITIES • GOLD experience 2ND EDITION **A2**

6A OUR TRAVEL PLANS

Student A

Travel plans	Camila From: Seville, Spain	Shan From: Beijing, China	Zoe From: Mexico City, Mexico
Country:	1	Russia	5 ....
Travel by:	plane	3	plane
Weather:	warm	4	6 ....
Travel time:	2	six days	four hours

Which country / Camilla / visit?   How long / journey / take?
How / Shan / travel?   What / weather / like?

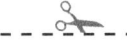

- -

Student B

Travel plans	Camila From: Seville, Spain	Shan From: Beijing, China	Zoe From: Mexico City, Mexico
Country:	Australia	3	Brazil
Travel by:	1	train	5 ....
Weather:	2	cold	hot
Travel time:	two days	4	6 ....

How / Camilla / travel?   What / weather / like?
Which country / Shan / visit?   How long / journey / take?

Photocopiable © Pearson Education Limited 2018   167

6B TRAVEL DOMINOES

car	sail a
plane	go by
train	drive a
helicopter	travel by
bike	catch a
coach	arrive at the
train station	get a
bus	go on
boat	fly a
foot	take the
car	travel by
tram	arrive at the
motorbike	travel by
underground	ride a
bike	fly a
port	go by
train	ride a
ferry	arrive at the
airport	travel by
ship	take the

PHOTOCOPIABLE ACTIVITIES

GOLD experience 2ND EDITION A2

6C A GREAT TRIP

Email

From: Charlotte
To: Emma
Subject: Trip to London

Hi Emma!

(1) I've got our tickets to London! They weren't the cheapest, but the journey will be really fast. We'll there in just two hours.

(2) We're not going to stay in the city centre. It's too expensive. We've got a nice apartment just outside the city.

(3) In the morning, we're going to see London the city in a really cool way. I hope you like boats – and travelling fast!

(4) I know a lovely café where we can go there for lunch. It's in the park and it isn't expensive. Their chocolate cake is the best!

(5) In the afternoon, we're going to the theatre to watch a film. I hope the weather is good because we'll be outside.

(6) In the evening we're going to a concert. It's not rock or pop music. It's something different.

See you soon!
Charlotte

Adverts

See the city by speedboat! Fast! Exciting! Cool!	**Big Purple Bus** Manchester to London £15	**City Cinema** Favourite films, great seats
Tour by bus See the sights Get on and off wherever you like!	**Express trains** From: Manchester To: London £105	**Films in the park** Come to our open-air cinema!
City Hotel A beautiful hotel in the centre of the city	**Classical concert** Amazing musicians from around the world	**Restaurant in the park** Excellent food from the world's best chefs
Prince Lane Apartment Comfortable apartment near the city	**Rock concert** Hear live bands!	**Park Café** Great meals and snacks

7A COULD YOU RIDE A BIKE?

Name	Skill	Now	Four years old
....	ride a bike	....	....
....	surf	....	....
....	play the guitar	....	....
....	play chess	....	....
....	....	....	....
....	....	....	....

Can you ride a bike? — Yes, I can.

Could you ride a bike when you were four years old? — No, I couldn't.

7B IN A SPIN

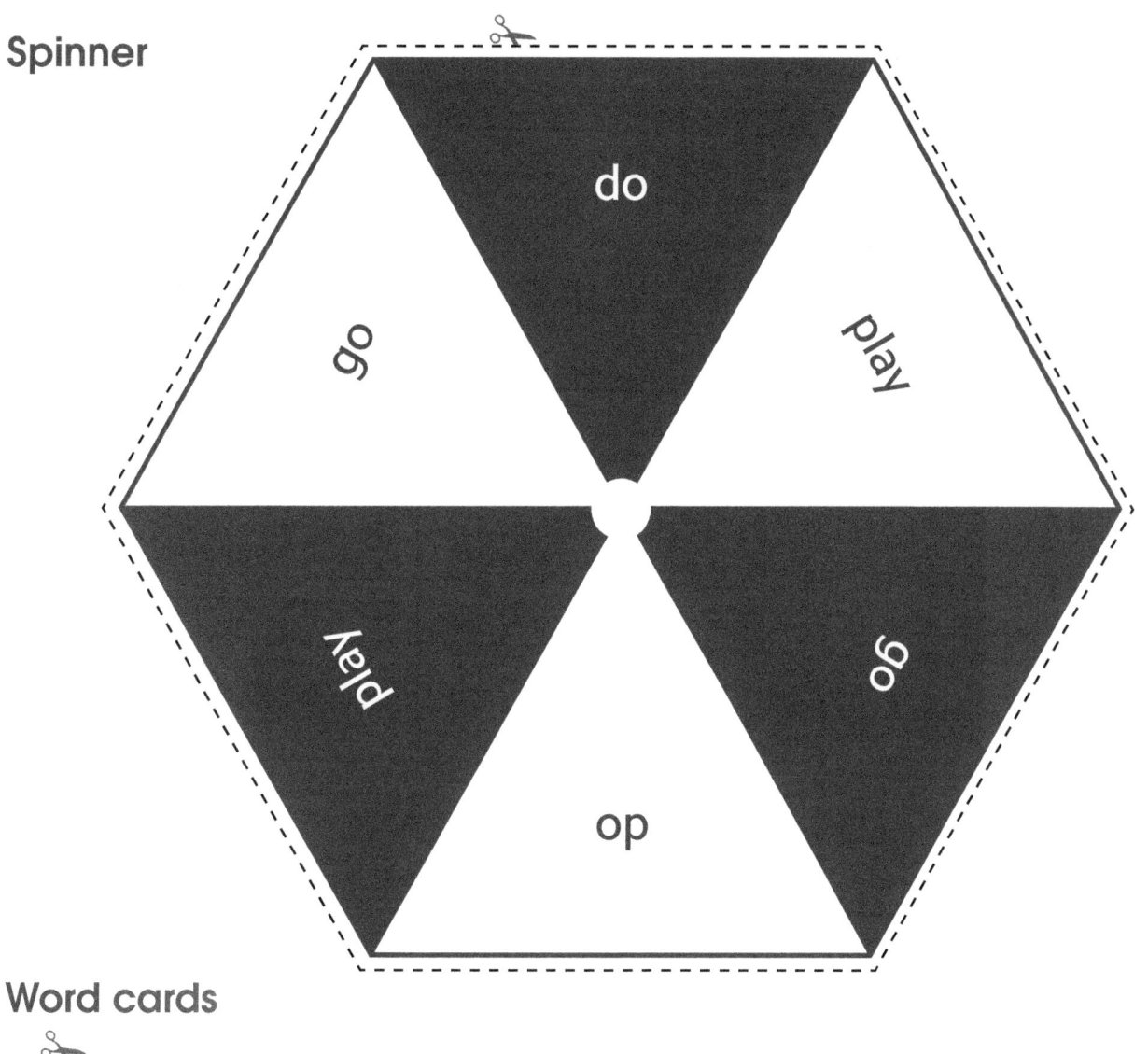

Spinner

do / play / go / do / go / play

Word cards

| skiing | surfing | football | exercise | swimming | basketball | tennis |
| cycling | badminton | diving | gymnastics | hockey | running | judo |

7C FIND THE ANSWERS

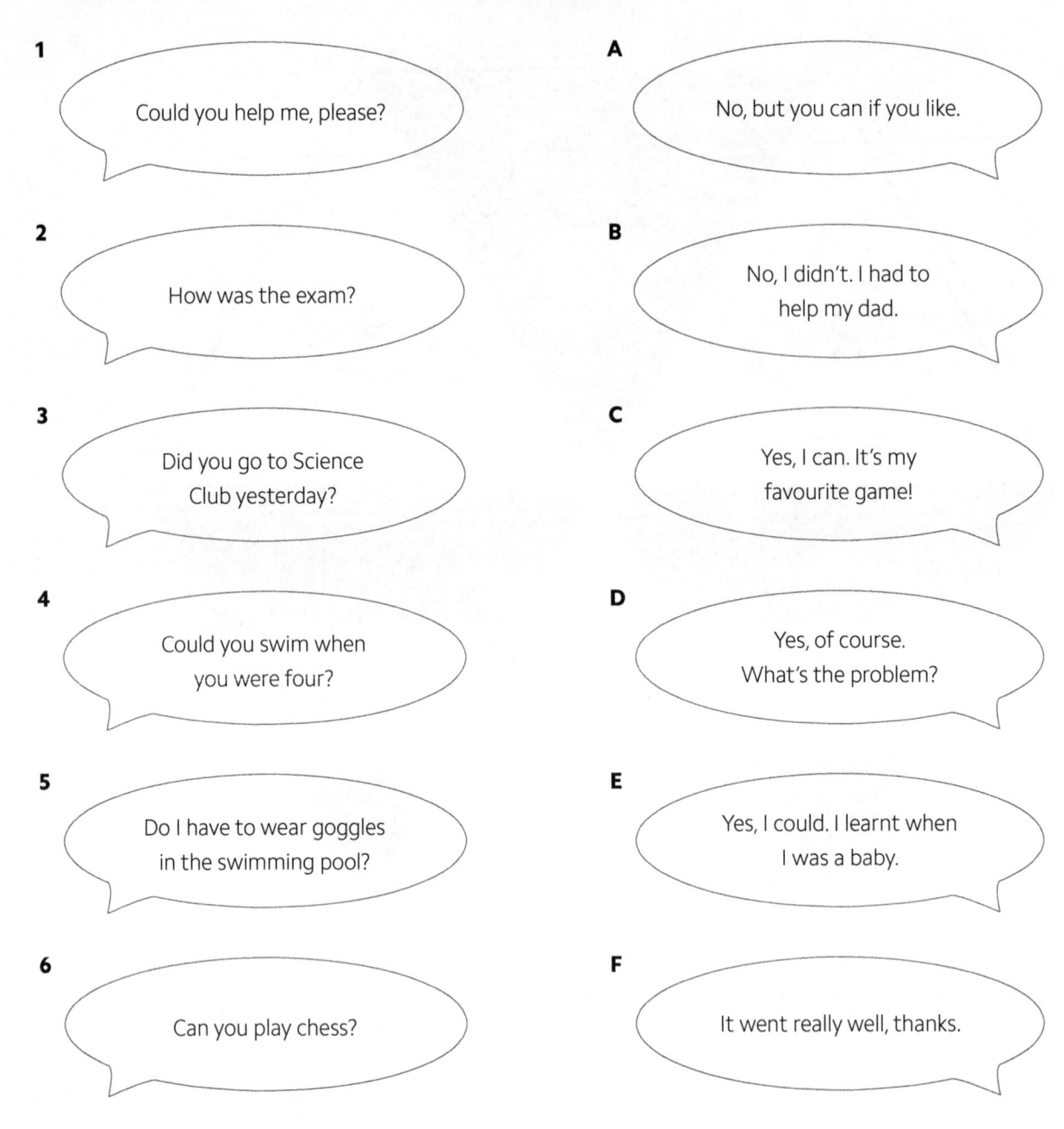

1. Could you help me, please?
2. How was the exam?
3. Did you go to Science Club yesterday?
4. Could you swim when you were four?
5. Do I have to wear goggles in the swimming pool?
6. Can you play chess?

A. No, but you can if you like.
B. No, I didn't. I had to help my dad.
C. Yes, I can. It's my favourite game!
D. Yes, of course. What's the problem?
E. Yes, I could. I learnt when I was a baby.
F. It went really well, thanks.

8A WHICH ANIMAL?

A

Continent: [1] .... (suAtairal)
I like hot, [2] .... (ryd) weather.
It's good to see the [3] .... (snu).
I have strong legs, but I can't walk.
I jump but never run.

B

Continents: South America, Antarctica, Australia
I usually live around the [1] .... (tosac),
Sometimes in [2] .... (wons) and
[3] .... (cie).
I'm a bird that doesn't fly.
But swimming can be nice!

C

Continents: every continent except Antarctica
A [1] .... (nariestrof) or desert can make a perfect home.
I lie rocks, so I get [2] .... (toh).
I don't like being [3] .... (dolc).

D

Continents: North America, South America,
[1] .... (rupEou), Asia
I don't mind cold weather.
My fur can keep me [2] .... (rawm).
I like to live in forests.
I hide when there's a [3] .... (morst).

E

Continents: Africa, Asia
I live in the [1] .... (sedret) where it's always very dry
I'm OK when it's [2] .... (lobiign) hot
or [3] .... (zeefring) cold at night.

F

Continents: every continent except
[1] .... (nAtcarcati)
I like to live in places where there are lots of trees, like forests, [2] ....s (sinald) and rainforests.
[3] .... (tHo) weather's best for me.

8B HAVE YOU EVER ... ?

Have you ever	ridden	a camel?
Have you ever	made	a video?
Have you ever	flown	in a helicopter?
Have you ever	swum	in a lake?
Have you ever	sung	at a concert?
Have you ever	written	a poem?
Have you ever	visited	a rainforest?
Have you ever	won	a competition?

8C HOLIDAY MESSAGES

Hi Ava,

I'm having a ¹.................... time in France. We're staying at a beautiful hotel near the beach. The weather is ².................... hot so it's great to go swimming in the sea. Yesterday we went an ³.................... restaurant for lunch. I had pancakes with chocolate sauce. I ⁴.................... French food! You can have surfing lessons at our hotel, so tomorrow, I'm going to learn to surf. I'm excited but I'm a ⁵.................... nervous, too. I hope I'm not really bad at it!

See you soon!
Becky

| amazing | bit | fantastic | love | very |

Good morning Dan,

I'm in Australia. We're staying in an ¹.................... in Sydney. I like it here. It's winter in Australia, so it isn't ².................... . It's warm today, but last night it was cold. I had a T-shirt and a jumper under my coat! The ³.................... from our apartment is nice. We can see the ⁴.................... and the bridge. It looks good. Today, we're going to climb it. It's high. I will be ⁵.................... !

Goodbye,
Alex

| apartment | sea | scared | hot | view |

9A ALL MIXED UP

A: What's your favourite meal?

B: I love steak and ¹**cereal**. What about you?

A: I like ²**boiled** chicken. It isn't healthy, but it's delicious.

A: What would you like for breakfast?

B: A bowl of ³**chips**, please.

A: I've just ⁴**barbecued** some bread. Would you like that, too?

A: Could you boil the ⁵**sandwich**, please? It's in a bag in the cupboard.

B: Yes, of course.

A: I'll make the ⁶**cake**. I've got the tomatoes here.

A: Could I have fish for dinner, please?

B: Would you like it with some nice green ⁷**biscuits**?

A: No, thank you. Could I have it with ⁸**fried** potatoes, please?

A: Sam's cooking outside.

B: Yes, he's just ⁹**baked** some burgers. Would you like one?

A: No, thanks. I'll just have a ¹⁰**salad**. Have you got any bread?

A: I'm going to bake a ¹¹**sauce**. Would you like to help?

B: Oh, yes, please. Can we bake some ¹²**pasta**, too?

9B WHAT SHOULD I DO?

I'm worried about my English test.	I've got a headache.	I want to make new friends.
I can't sleep.	I can't do my homework.	I want to learn how to cook.
I've got too much work to do.	I want to be healthier.	My school marks aren't good.
I'm bored at weekends.	I feel sick!	I want to speak English better.
I've got stomach ache.	I'm always tired.	I've got toothache.
I want to exercise, but I don't like team sports.	I want to be better at football.	I've got a cold.

9C THE RACE

1	It was the last week of term	....	there was a race at Aisha's school.
2	Aisha wanted to win	....	she was the best runner.
3	At the start of the race Aisha was winning,	....	then her friend, Lola, fell over.
4	Aisha wanted to help her friend	....	she stopped running.
5	Aisha sat with Lola	....	the teacher looked at her leg.
6	Lola's leg wasn't broken	....	she stayed at school.
7	Aisha helped Lola to the classroom	....	she couldn't walk easily.
8	Another girl won the race,	....	Aisha didn't mind.